ADVENTURES IN DISRUPTION

ADVENTURES IN DISRUPTION

How to Start, Survive, and Succeed as a Creative Entrepreneur

SAM AQUILLANO

BUSINESS
DESIGN
SCHOOL

Business Design School books may be purchased in bulk at special discounts for sales promotion, corporate gifts, fundraising, or educational purposes. Special editions can also be created to specifications. For details contact info@businessdesignschool.org.

Published by Business Design School.

businessdesignschool.org

Print ISBN: 979-8-9896363-0-3
eBook ISBN: 979-8-9896363-1-0
Audiobook ISBN: 979-8-9896363-2-7

To Nicole, who taught me
how to follow my heart.

CONTENTS

By Michael DiTullo

There are a lot of books about startups and entrepreneurship, why should you read this one? Read this book because Sam Aquillano has the courage to tell you the candid, unvarnished truth about how hard it is to start something and why you shouldn't let that stop you. It would have been so easy for Sam to have never left his corporate design job at Bose. Working at a company like that is a coveted position for any industrial designer. He could have stayed and lived a happy life, but that just wasn't an option. I know it wasn't because I was in that same position. I was a designer at one of the most well-known companies in the world, Nike, and I was very happy there. There was just this little itch at the back of my mind that would never seem to go away. At a certain point, I knew I would have to leave to start my own company even though in many ways I didn't want to. I just had to.

Do you have that feeling? Of course you do. You wouldn't be reading this if you didn't. One of the biggest secrets that Sam lets you in on in this book is that there are many people out there with the same feeling you have. The sense that they could build something no one else has ever built before, that they could fly on their own. Find a few other people like yourself and start something. Not because it will be easy, it won't be, but because you just have to fly.

American philosopher, artist, and publisher Elbert Hubbard once said, "A little more persistence, a little more effort, and what seemed hopeless failure may turn to glorious success." This book is all about persistence, not of one person, but of a group of people, all bonded to a common cause. If you start something, you will need that group of people that are more than friends, they are more than partners; they are fellow adventurers who will never let you give up. There will be times when the going will get tough, you will have doubts, and there will be challenges that will force you to change course and make a new plan. Having those like-minded individuals around you will ensure there is always someone there ready to keep pushing. What you are about to read is a first-hand account of Sam and his team's journey that will include the trials they faced, the lessons they learned, and tips for you to use in your own journey.

You might have noticed the word "creative" right in front of "entrepreneur" on the cover. You might not be a designer, a copywriter, or an engineer; but if you are an entrepreneur, you are creative. By definition, your goal is to create something that never existed, so you will need to be in that creative head space. Sam is about to tell you how he and his team used low-stakes creative approaches at every turn to take safe risks, try things out—even if just for themselves—and how they turned the people they were pitching to into believers. When your vision becomes their vision, you win.

"To read is to voyage through time."
— Carl Sagan, author, astronomer

"How does someone start a museum?"

I was sitting across from one of my students, Billy Vespa, in a hotel ballroom at a design conference in the fall of 2009, and I had just told him my big idea. He was one of the first people with whom I shared my business idea, even though it had been rattling around in my brain for over two years. But he asked the right question at the right moment. My friend and long-time collaborator, Derek Cascio, and I were just ending our tenure as volunteer leaders of the Boston chapter of a national design organization, and Billy knew Derek and I were not likely to sit idle for long.

He asked me what we were going to do next: "I know you and Derek always have something cooking." Indeed we did, I told him: "Our plan is to start a design museum here in Boston."

"How does someone start a museum?" he asked. I replied, "I have no idea."

But over thirteen years, and with a lot of help, we launched and built Design Museum Everywhere, a new kind of museum to bring the transformative power of design everywhere—and I mean everywhere. Over the course of our entrepreneurial adventure, we redefined what it means to be a museum in the 21st century. We're online, nomadic, and accessible to all. Instead of a single museum location, we pop up exhibitions and special events in places like galleries, retail environments, public spaces, lobbies, schools, and more in cities across the country. And we're everywhere you find content: virtual events, online articles, podcasts, videos, and even a quarterly print magazine on design impact. We disrupted the entire notion of what a museum is. In place of a building, we built a global community of design thinkers and changemakers. It was the ultimate adventure in creative entrepreneurship.

Creative entrepreneurship is the pursuit of launching and growing not just new businesses but new *kinds* of businesses— sometimes the business model hasn't even been invented yet! Creative ventures require creative thinking, problem solving, and the ability to identify and capitalize on opportunities.

I was once pitched by a marketing consulting firm that thought they could help take Design Museum Everywhere to the next level. The big case study they showed as proof was their work for a company that sold yachts. It was an impressive presentation if you had a simple business model, like selling yachts. I had to explain to them the complex quilt of business models we employ at the museum. A mix of membership, advertising, subscriptions, ticket sales, sponsorship, grants, and donations—each revenue stream with its own unique variations needed to be woven together into the beautiful patchwork that is our business model. But that's what it takes for creative ventures to survive and succeed.

Think about Airbnb. A model for creating a business where individuals rent out their homes or apartments to travelers just didn't exist until co-founders Brian Chesky and Joe Gebbia—two industrial designers—made it happen. They were living in San Francisco in 2008, struggling to pay their rent, when the Industrial Designers Society of America international conference came to town, and they realized designers attending the conference (including me) needed a cheap place to stay. So they set up a website called AirBed & Breakfast, and the first listings were the three air mattresses set up in their living room. From there they went on to disrupt the entire hotel industry.

Then there's ArtLifting, started by my friend Liz Powers and her brother Spencer. ArtLifting is a social enterprise that empowers artists who are houseless or have disabilities by selling their artwork and providing them with a source of income. Liz studied art therapy, and while volunteering at shelters, she noticed many of the residents were talented artists, but they lacked the means to sell their work. ArtLifting was created as a platform for these artists to sell their artwork and earn a fair wage. Now that's life-changing, disruptive innovation!

Creative entrepreneurs like Brian, Joe, Liz, and Spencer are driven by their passion for impact, change, and bringing new ideas to life. You are a creative entrepreneur as well. Even if you won't admit it to yourself (yet), I know it's true. I know you have a business idea—or two or three—in that head of yours. I know because you're human, and our natural inclination is to create, to make, and to build. But starting something is hard, risky, and clouded in uncertainty.

Entrepreneurship can be so overwhelming with endless possibilities that most ideas stay locked in people's minds alongside self-doubt and worry—denying the rest of us their impactful creations.

Now imagine a world where you have launched your dream business idea. Imagine you broke through self-doubt, recruited people to your cause, proved the naysayers wrong, and built something incredible that brings people joy and utility and makes real change in the world—something you can be proud of. That's a pretty great world. I like living in that world, the land of possibilities. When you're in that time and space of utilizing your passion, collaborating with partners, and offering something to people they truly value, it's magical.

I hope my entrepreneurial story can serve as a guide. I'll share the real story, not a glossy, spruced-up startup mythology. You'll hear how I deliberately got my idea out of my head and shared it with others, even if it took over two years; how my co-founder, Derek, and I built a community from day one; how we pivoted constantly and maintained a culture of adaptability to find and create opportunities every step of the way. I'll add some insights and advice along the way so you can apply what you learn and accelerate past the mistakes I made.

I wrote this tale of our journey because over the course of the thirteen years I ran the Design Museum as its founding executive director, I got a lot of questions just like Billy Vespa's: "How did you start the Design Museum?" I've sat across from so many aspiring entrepreneurs over the years—in coffee shops, Zoom meetings, and classrooms at Babson College, Wentworth Institute of Technology, and

Massachusetts College of Art and Design where I taught design and entrepreneurship—and shared this story.

Folks who know me know I live and breathe design—I consider it my calling, and I'll share how I found it and combined it with my entrepreneurial nature and business acumen to create new initiatives. But let me be clear—I didn't start the Design Museum alone. Without the dedication of countless individuals, this story wouldn't be possible. This isn't a quick path to success with a ten-step plan for launching your new idea. And I'm not here to pretend any of this was easy—that's not real.

I do believe that every new business has three foundational assets: your team, your community, and your brand. Your team believes in the business, supports you, and makes more things possible than you could ever hope to do alone. With a team, one plus one equals three (or more). You'll read about my co-founder and our team in chapter two. A community believes in you, feels deeply connected to your vision, and will evangelize the business to the world—every business needs a community to help lift it out of obscurity, and I'll show you how we built ours in chapter three. Your brand is how you present your venture to the world. It's visual, yes, but it's more than a logo. It's how the essence of your work permeates everything you do, and it's what sticks in the mind of your customers, bringing them back for more. Brand is so important you'll read about it in chapters one and three, and in chapter eight I share the unique way we developed our brand identity.

Of course, every business also needs to make money. In chapter ten, I go into detail on how we monetized our unique approach into a sustainable business model. Finally, in chapters twelve and thirteen, you'll see how we achieved product-market fit and grew our business and value to our community.

I promise an interesting, insightful, real story about the entrepreneurial adventure that resulted in a creative, disruptive organization. I hope it inspires you to make your business idea come to life. Let's start at the beginning—the real beginning—when the idea for Design Museum Everywhere was just a dream stuck in my head. Here's how I got it out.

CHAPTER 1

Survive the Commencement Paradox

You are the first customer for your own idea.

"The hardest thing about getting started, is getting started"
— Guy Kawasaki, author, entrepreneur, and evangelist

When is the beginning? You might think it's at the start, but no. When we're talking about launching an idea, business, organization, venture, you name it, the beginning and the start are much more complicated. Take this book for example. The process of writing this book began in June 2014 when I was invited to speak at TEDxFenway about the museum I founded, Design Museum Boston (now called Design Museum Everywhere, but more on that later). At the time, TEDx events were popping up around the world as independently organized versions of the main, very exclusive, annual TED conference. As the founder of a growing startup, I was honored to speak, and I knew that any opportunity to talk about my business in front of an audience of any size was something to lean into. The event organizers invited me to talk about the Design

Speaking about Design Museum Boston at TEDxBoston, 2013.

Museum, but I had something else on my mind: helping others get to the same place I was, having started something I was super passionate about and working like hell to make it survive and succeed.

I was introduced to the TEDxFenway stage by Anita Walker, Executive Director of the Massachusetts Cultural Council. She said something like, "Please welcome Sam Aquillano to talk to us about a new kind of museum he has started." I got on stage in front of a few hundred people and proceeded to let them know, "Actually, I won't be talking about Design Museum Boston, at least not directly." Out of the corner of my eye, I saw the organizers' faces turn white (sorry, organizers). I proceeded to remind everyone about the theme of the event, grit, and that the grittiest thing I could think of was entrepreneurship. I proceeded to give my talk, titled, "The Laws of Zero-Stage Entrepreneurship." In that short, eleven-minute presentation, I gave ten bits of advice for starting a business, particularly a business that no one thought could ever exist. Those ten points pretty closely match the chapters of this book.

I finished my talk, and as I walked offstage, I knew in my gut that I should write a book about my experience starting Design Museum Everywhere and provide advice for new entrepreneurs. But it took me seven years to start writing it— why? It would be easy to say a lot happened and got in the way of launching this publishing venture. In the seven years since I gave that talk, I got married, had three kids, bought a house, and grew a startup nonprofit museum to a level of sustainability and impact of which I never could have dreamed—these are important reasons, but they're beside the point. The truth is it took me seven years to convince myself that I should do this, that I had something to say and contribute to this space, and that my experiences could be helpful to others. I was filled with fear and self-doubt, and I didn't follow the advice I'm writing in this book for you (I wish I had!).

Business, particularly *starting* a business, is one of the most complex things there is. But when you boil it down, you realize a lot of business is about convincing people to do something— convincing people to join you (hiring), convincing people you have the right strategy (leadership), and convincing people to buy what you're selling (marketing and sales). But as so often happens in the stories of entrepreneurship we tell each other, we gloss over the internal struggle. Starting something is deeply personal, and the first person you need to convince is yourself. You are your own first customer of this new idea. Are you going to buy in?

I didn't buy into my own idea immediately. For me, there was a sizable gap between the beginning and the start.

To understand the beginning of the Design Museum, you need to understand more about me. I was a creative kid from two creative parents—surrounded by a big Italian-American family that prioritizes family and community. My dad began his career as a draftsman before succeeding in corporate finance. My mom is incredibly creative and can do wondrous things with arts and crafts. My parents supported my earliest creative endeavors and showed me the value of hard work. My mom taught me how to draw and helped me and my siblings enter the annual Parent Teacher Association youth art contest every year. I won the state trophy in fifth grade—a very proud moment for a ten-year-old artist finding his creative place in the world.

I've always been entrepreneurial. In elementary school, I sold baseball cards to the other kids on the bus. When I was thirteen, I got a spiral-bound notebook and wrote "Book of Ideas" on the cover. On the first page, I wrote, "I'm going to change the world." I filled that notebook with ideas for products, businesses, video games, and more. In high school, I got one of the first consumer CD burners—I handed out little slips of paper at school with ten lines on them. My classmates could list any ten songs, and I'd make them a mix CD for $10. (Not the most legal business. I understand that now.) And all through my teenage years, my brother Steve and I ran a lawn and landscaping business called Earthworks Lawn Care.

I was a creative entrepreneur before I knew what that meant. As a junior in high school, I had no idea design was a potential career, I didn't even know "design" was a thing. I knew I liked to draw and come up with ideas and make them happen. Not knowing about design, I toured colleges and universities around New England, New York, and Pennsylvania, looking at mechanical engineering departments. My parents and I thought engineering was my best bet at a career doing something I enjoyed and was good at. No offense to the mechanical engineers of the world, but it wasn't my cup of tea. As I heard presentations from faculty and got tours from engineering students, there just wasn't enough art or creativity—I needed something different. It was the last school I visited with my parents, Rochester Institute of Technology (RIT), where I made the discovery that would change my life. We toured the engineering department, of course, and I felt that same feeling of dread—was this all the world and the economy had for me?

But it was in the financial aid office, as my parents were discussing options with a staffer, that I found it. Sitting in the waiting area, there was a big display of pamphlets to my right —a pamphlet for each major at the college. And there it was, a pamphlet with some products on the front and a sketch of an ice boat. I didn't even know what an ice boat was. I grabbed it, opened it, and proceeded to read about the field of industrial design, where designers work to envision the form and function of the products we all see and use every day. I had struck gold. This was it. I only applied to RIT, mistakenly thinking that RIT was the only school on the entire East Coast that offered industrial design.

I struck gold twice because it was also at RIT where I first met Derek Cascio—a lifelong friend and the person with whom I would start the Design Museum. Derek is truly one of a kind. He's not a large person (quite the opposite, he's a skinny Italian guy). He's bald, although he did have hair when we first met, with a beard. He has more energy in his pinky finger than a normal person expends in a typical year. He's fueled by coffee—I rarely see him without a paper cup in his hand, and he's one of the best designers I know. He can design and draw anything and tell you the story behind things that only exist in his imagination. Watching Derek's Instagram live sessions, where he narrates as he draws products, robots, and monsters is now one of my favorite pastimes. My kids love it, too.

Derek simultaneously believes people should be responsible and take care of their own business *and* that he can help every human with whatever they need. If Derek had a tagline, it would be, "I'm here to help." As a kid, he was always drawing characters and developing stories, so when it came time for college, he enrolled in the top-tier animation program at RIT. With him in animation and me in industrial design, our paths didn't cross in the classroom. My roommate in the cramped RIT dorms, however, was in animation, and Derek would swing by to chat with Anthony about classes and assignments from time to time. Derek told me later that he was always looking over my shoulder as I was sketching a product or making a little foam model—he was intrigued by design. That year, Derek sort of realized animation wasn't enough for him. He wanted more, so he transferred out of RIT and moved to Boston to look for other academic opportunities and be closer to home. I didn't think I'd ever see him again.

———

At RIT I launched my first entrepreneurial effort in design. During my junior year, I and a handful of fellow design students—Don Lehman, Laura "Ori" Fowler, and Chuck Cerankosky—were on the road from Rochester, NY, to Bridgeport, CT, in Don's old, blue minivan. And we were

18

excited. The Industrial Design Society of America's annual national conference was completely out of reach for students and young designers, owing to the ticket cost and travel required. But the regional conferences took place at design schools in each region and were billed as an accessible way to connect to a community of designers in your area. And they were (supposedly) designed to support the next generation of designers, students.

That was us, on our way to Bridgeport in Don's minivan, eyes wide and ready to be wowed by our first experience at an IDSA regional conference. What we were met with, however, was a lackluster experience that didn't cater to our needs as design students. The presentations were boring, on topics that didn't concern us, and the structure of the event made it hard to network and meet people. We wanted to learn and connect, but instead, we were stuck listening to content that didn't matter to us and waiting in long lines for portfolio reviews.

There was one presentation we didn't want to miss. Cameron Sinclair was the closing keynote speaker, slated to talk about his organization, Architecture for Humanity, and how he was using design to change the world. That was something and someone we wanted to see. The problem was the conference organizers planned the student portfolio review at the same time as the closing keynote presentation. We had to choose—and we were all looking for summer internships, so we waited in the long line to have our portfolios reviewed and missed Cameron's presentation.

On the drive back to Rochester, we were livid with complaints. We wasted our time and money. This wasn't the first conference marketed toward design students that left us wanting. After a lot of complaining from Don, Ori, and I, there was a prolonged silence, then Don spoke up: "We should just do our own conference." We all agreed. We spent the rest of the long drive dreaming about what a design conference by students for students could be like. We each built off each other's passion and energy, and by the time we got back to campus, the plan was set, and it felt inevitable. The three of us were going to start a new design conference.

What followed was the three of us working together to create something from nothing. Sometimes, all it takes to get started is a group of friends who agree that something could be done better. We divided up all the work to start and execute a student-led conference—visioning, branding, fundraising, planning, coordination, marketing, production, and more. There was so much to do, and not one of us could do it alone. We trusted each other to make it happen. The result? In less than a year, we developed, launched, and produced a three-day design conference called Thought at Work with keynote presenters, workshops, and portfolio reviews. It was a huge success. We even had Cameron Sinclair join us for the closing keynote. In the end, we got to see, and meet, him after all. Thought at Work still exists to this day as an annual student design conference at RIT, and it all started with three friends, three co-founders, working together to make it real.

———————

Between Thought at Work and my regular coursework, I took design school extremely seriously—design was my calling after all, and I had something to prove. I worked so hard. Too hard. I achieved a perfect 4.0-grade point average and was named RIT's student merit award winner after presenting my portfolio. Winning this honor meant I went on to present my portfolio at the regional conference of the Industrial Designers Society of America.

In 2004, the Northeast Conference was at MassArt in Boston. So Don, Ori, our classmates, and I, along with some of the RIT industrial Design faculty, traveled to Boston for the event. During one of the talks, I looked down the row, and who do I see? Derek Cascio. We both greeted each other with the same look: what the hell are you doing here? We got to talking after the session and learned that Derek really had been watching me work on my industrial design homework. When he transferred, he ended up at MassArt, studying industrial design.

During that conference I was recruited to work at Bose Corporation after graduation, designing consumer electronics outside of Boston. I moved to the city shortly after finishing RIT, and from that point on, Derek and I were pretty much inseparable.

I was in my early twenties, and I had made it—at least, it felt like I had. I had a career in industrial design, one that I never could have imagined when I first found a pamphlet about majoring in design. To be designing consumer electronics that hundreds of thousands of people use to enjoy music every day was a dream. For anyone who loves design and music, imagine combining them into one job and mixing it with some of the best technology in the world. It was a great job, and if you stuck with it at Bose, you were set for life: Bose overpaid to retain staff. They had amazing retirement benefits, and they even had a pension program. I loved my job, and I was good at it.

But I found out pretty quickly that simply working as a designer wasn't enough for me. The corporate world (at least the one I was in) didn't take kindly to a young entrepreneurial designer. I would float business and product ideas to leadership, and even though my ideas were celebrated within the design department, product leadership at Bose had the attitude that if they didn't come up with the idea, it wasn't a good one.

On top of that, I found I had passions equal to design in things like community and education, which I tried to pursue within my job. Without being asked, I would plan staff team-building gatherings off-campus, and I would find ways to learn new skills and apply them in different departments. I once weaseled my way into a year-long customer research effort where we interviewed hundreds of people in their homes about their audio products—my manager didn't know I was doing it until he saw my name on the front cover of the report. My main job wasn't enough. To scratch the itches of design, entrepreneurship, community, and education, I had to add some extracurricular activities.

In college, I led our student chapter of the Industrial Designers Society of America. For me, it was a way to build my network both within design school and in the industry. I wanted to meet the design thought leaders that I hoped to learn from (and someday work for and with), so I would plan events and invite them to speak or exhibit their work. I'd get to meet them, and my fellow students and I would benefit from them sharing their ideas and expertise. Everybody wins! Plus I got to incorporate my love of entrepreneurship (our little chapter was like a startup), community, and education.

I continued my involvement with IDSA after graduation during my years working at Bose. For over six years, along with my fellow chapter leaders Derek, Bruce Lee, Sara Stump, and Shannon Buono, we planned conferences, mentoring sessions for design students, workshops, and small exhibitions. And during that time I was fortunate to meet so many amazing designers, and learn directly from them—folks I now consider friends and supporters of my work to this day. I wanted to build a huge network in the design world so that I could generate and take advantage of any opportunities that came my way.

One such opportunity came when Sam Montague, Department Chair of the Industrial Design Department at Wentworth Institute of Technology (WIT), began searching for an adjunct professor to teach consumer electronic design. At that point in my career, I thought teaching was something I would do in my later years after I gained more experience. But when a colleague of mine at Bose, Kevin Krauss, suggested I connect with Sam at Wentworth, something clicked for me.

Here was a chance to teach design the way I wished it had been taught to me—I had an amazing experience at RIT, but there's always room for improvement. It was also a chance to grow my network—design students eventually become designers. It was a chance to hone a new skill, teaching, and this played right into my love of education. And finally, I'd be earning extra money, always a good thing. Once I got into the classroom in the evening at WIT, I was in love—I loved planning my lectures and skill demonstrations, I loved seeing the students work hard, and it was so fun giving them critiques and pointers to take things to the next level. I was officially hooked.

———————

I was trying so hard to fit all my passions into my one life. I was working full-time as a corporate industrial designer during the day at Bose; at night, two to four times a week, I would teach industrial design at Wentworth Institute of Technology; all the while, I was the Boston Chapter Chair of the Industrial Designers Society of America, planning around twelve community events per year. It was a lot, but I loved it and relished the opportunity to be able to work hard at what I loved.

Working as a designer, teaching design, and running a design community—these three elements of my career put me in a unique position to observe some interesting factors about the world of design. At the time, folks in design were very much rooted in their design field silos—design communities were homogenous. Industrial designers with industrial designers, graphic designers with graphic designers, architects with architects, and so on. Each field had at least one major professional organization that united the field, advocated for good design within that field, and provided some level of community and professional development for practicing designers. I had the Industrial Designers Society of America as my professional organization. There was also the American Institute for Architects, the American Institute of Graphic Arts, the American Society of Interior Designers, and on and on. I didn't love that designers were separated by field; I wanted to connect and learn from all different types of designers—certainly, there were aspects of the work that transcended specific disciplines.

I also didn't see anyone, or any organization, engaging the general public in conversations about good design. Companies like Apple, Target, and IKEA started using the word "design" in their marketing and were building their brands around good, accessible design, but no one was educating the public about design. This hit home for me before my career in design even began. When I told my parents I wanted to be an industrial designer, they had no idea what that was or what I was talking about. And when they learned that I'd need to go to "art school" to get a design degree, the warning bells sounded.

Design wasn't yet in the popular lexicon in the U.S. At one point, I was in a factory supporting the first run of manufacturing for one of the products I designed. I noticed a group of people sorting products into two piles for shipment. I asked why they were sorting. They informed me they were looking for units where the parts fit perfectly and there were zero defects—those would be shipped and displayed in stores throughout Europe and Asia. The units in the other pile looked okay but weren't perfect. Those were headed for—you guessed it—the United States, where presumably folks had lower design sensibilities than the rest of the world. That didn't sit right.

Around this same time, I was visiting various design museums around the world. I've always enjoyed the immersive environment of museums. Whether it was the nature center in my hometown of Erie, PA, or the Museum of Science in Boston, I really enjoy getting lost in learning while being surrounded by people and beautiful spaces. On a trip to New York City, I visited the Cooper Hewitt National Design Museum. When my sister Kate studied abroad in London, I visited and toured the London Design Museum. And when the Bose design team won an award from the Red Dot Design Museum in Essen, Germany, I was there. Being in these spaces energized me. Here were these monuments to design, and they were open to the public! It hit me: design is for everyone, and museums are for everyone, too.

One evening in 2007, I came home from work, and all of these thoughts were swirling in my head. *Designers are in silos based on their individual disciplines, not connecting with each other across fields. Very little design engagement with the public beyond some corporate marketing campaigns and a few design museums scattered around the world. Me in Boston, working, teaching, and connecting with designers in a city filled with beautiful museums.* That evening, I pulled out my laptop and googled "Boston Design Museum." That was the beginning—the moment the idea went from liquid to crystallized in my mind.

Based on Google's search algorithm, I only found the websites for many of the design museums I'd already visited. I saw a handful of Boston-based design professional organizations, even IDSA. But there wasn't much, if anything, about a design museum in Boston. On the third page of results, I found an obscure discussion board where someone had posted that they would love to see a design museum open in Boston, a city with so much design history, talent, and companies. The conversation looked to have been going on for a while, with other folks agreeing it was a great idea and that it should happen.

I read the entire discussion board from beginning to end—every comment. Then I read it again. Maybe this was something people wanted. It may seem insignificant in the bigger picture, but that random discussion board did give me an important boost of confidence, but not too much confidence. I would read and re-read that same discussion board—never adding my own voice—for two years.

Was I the person to start a design museum in Boston? I was 25 years old, I had a lot of energy, and I was certainly gaining experience in design, education, and community. Plus, I was building the network of contacts that it would take to do something like this. Deep down, I knew I could start a business. I'd done it before, but never at this scale. Would a design museum in Boston be successful? Would it be a huge mistake to spend my time and money on something like this? I had to try and convince myself that this was the right (or wrong) thing to do. I was the first potential customer of my own idea.

————

The first stage of entrepreneurship is typically called early-stage. At this point in my journey, I wasn't even at early-stage, I was at zero-stage; meaning there was nothing but my pure idea and me, ready to be convinced that I should move forward and make it real.

I'll admit, I had a bit of a fire under me—I really liked the idea of starting a design museum in Boston. It seemed like the perfect fit for my passions and skillset. I thought a lot about my Book of Ideas—that little notebook I wrote my ideas in as a kid—and how for years I watched from the sidelines as the ideas I wrote in my spiral-bound book became real, created by others. I learned the hard lesson early that an idea is not enough. It's all about what you do with that idea, when and how you execute it.

Perhaps ridiculously, and without any scientific fact, I now believe that since there are eight billion people on Earth, at least ten other people are having the same idea as you at that same moment somewhere in the world. This belief was at least partially true in my mind because I was reading and re-reading an online discussion board of folks who also had an idea for a design museum in Boston.

I began consciously and subconsciously working to convince myself that this was an idea to move forward on and that I was the one to do it. The first thing I did was name the museum—when you name something, you make it real, even if just in your mind. I named the museum Design Museum Boston—because there's a Design Museum London, and it's okay to emulate others, especially in the zero-stage.

I started designing logos for this fictitious museum, and I photoshopped the logos onto photos of buildings to make the museum seem real to me. I even made fake business cards and letterheads for Design Museum Boston. These important, early visualizations prompted me to think about what my life could be like if I started Design Museum Boston.

I know now that I was practicing something elite athletes do all the time. Athletes at the top of their game routinely visualize, or use mental imagery of what a successful performance, game, race, or match will look and feel like. They do this over and over to build the mental image and muscle memory that allows them to push themselves in the key moments of competition. Sports psychologist Dr. Jim Taylor refers to using mental imagery as "weight lifting for the mind." All my mental imagery—my thoughts and dreams—was bent in one direction. Seeing the Design Museum and my life with it in my mind's eye was making it real for me and helping convince myself to move forward.

———

What's your idea? How can you convince your first customer (you) to move forward? Start with yourself. Unless you have way more courage than me, sharing your idea with others immediately is a terrifying prospect. Try to make it real for yourself, visualize it any way you can. As Dr. Daniel Siegel says, "Name it to tame it." If you want to start a subscription mail-order cupcake shop, give it a name, and it will instantly feel more real to you. It doesn't have to be the final name—you can change it, but *For Cupcakes' Sake* has a nice ring to it.

Make a logo for your brand, even if you're not a graphic designer. Figure out a way to create something. Again, this doesn't need to be the final logo—in fact, I recommend *not* making this the final logo for your company. This is about moving fast, and it's just for you. There are plenty of free online tools and services to make logos. Use the logo for yourself—you don't have to show anyone, but in the case of our mail-order cupcake shop, I would recommend you get a gift box, fill it with your delicious cupcakes, print out the logo, cut it out, and glue it to the top of the box. Now, you're holding your product. It's rough, but who cares? It's like you are playing business make-believe. But you're not just pretending—you're visualizing.

Beyond visualization, I recommend gaining some relevant experience associated with your idea. Maybe you're already in the industry or field in which you're going to start your venture. If not, there are ways to tangentially gain experience. For me, it was starting the Thought at Work conference in college and running the local chapter of the Industrial Designers Society of America in Boston. I knew how to design things, but volunteering for the IDSA gave me a chance to be entrepreneurial, run a chapter of a nonprofit, manage a budget, build community, and deliver programmings like events and exhibitions—all things I wasn't doing in my design job but that I would need to do at Design Museum Boston.

For your budding cupcake business idea, maybe this means getting a part-time job in a local bakery on the weekends to learn how to scale from your at-home kitchen to a more customer-facing model. Or maybe you've got the baking thing down, and you should volunteer at your local food pantry to witness perishable food distribution at scale.

My wife Nicole wanted to be (and successfully became) a full-time ceramic artist. To gain studio experience she took the same evening adult education course at Massachusetts College of Art and Design over and over and over for years—this gave her access to the kilns and equipment needed to hone her craft, but more importantly, it granted access into the twice-annual art sales at the college where she could try to sell her work to customers. This takes time, but trust me, it's worth it. You'll be working at the bakery or volunteering at the food pantry, but you'll be thinking about how your business will run. It's an investment in time that will pay off.

On top of all the visualization and experience-gathering, think about and write about what your life will be like if you start this venture, and it's successful. This could purely be a thought exercise, but I do recommend writing it down or even typing something in your phone's notes app. Putting it down "on paper," just like naming it, making a logo, etc., makes it real. And when you write it down, you can go back to it again and again as you feel those moments of self-doubt that will slow you down. While you're doing the work to convince yourself to move forward, you're also convincing yourself to share your idea or your plan with others—and that's critical to really starting up.

———————

The beginning of Design Museum Boston was a quiet notion in my mind that evolved into very loud internal conversations to convince myself to share my vision out loud. That might not be a compelling founding story to share, but I encourage every entrepreneur not to gloss over the reality of this internal struggle. I think we're either too caught up in the hero narrative or too self-conscious to share all the fear and self-doubt that naturally exists at the beginning. In reality, this first part of starting something happens in our own minds, as a pure vision mixed with confusion and hesitancy—and that's okay. This is a real part of the process, whether we choose to admit it or not. People talk about taking a massive leap into entrepreneurship; in reality, it's many leaps. This is just the first one. It's okay to wrestle with whether or not to take the first leap—convince yourself and get ready to convince a lot of other people. Chances are, you're going to need help.

CHAPTER 2

Identify Unconditional Support

You're going to need it.

"It's better to have no cofounder than to have a bad cofounder, but it's still bad to be a solo founder."

— Sam Altman, former president, Y-Combinator, CEO, OpenAI

I've never started a business alone. Whether it was Earthworks Lawn Care with my brother Steve, or launching the Thought at Work conference with Don, Ori, and a big group of our fellow students at RIT, I was always part of a team of co-founders and collaborators.

There's an old saying: "If you want to go fast, go alone. If you want to go far, go together." I believe that holds true in your creative startup. Experts believe this saying originated from somewhere in Africa, though they're not sure from where or by whom. No matter its origins, this saying offers a certain contrast to the rugged individualism proselytized in the United

States, where *going it alone* and *self-reliance* and *me not we* are the celebrated norm. Going it alone is a problem because your business idea is more complex than you realize right now. And that's okay. If you think too much about the utter complexity of launching your business, you might stop, and I just finished helping you convince yourself that this is the right thing to do! Push those thoughts of complexity out of your head, but whatever your business idea is, it's too complex for one person to get it off the ground alone. You need a co-founder.

I'm not going to say going it alone is impossible, but I don't recommend it—you need the support, people who are with you all the way and can help shoulder the burden of early-stage entrepreneurship. You've convinced yourself to take on and launch this new venture, but how are you going to convince hundreds of people to join your community or movement, or thousands to buy your product or service, if you can't convince just one other person to join you on this adventure?

———

There I was with a best friend and collaborator, and I hadn't shared this idea with him in two years. Derek and I are close. Back then, we were spending so much time together that we practically had our own language. My brother even made a joke during his speech at my wedding that I spoke with Derek more than my mother and wife combined.

Derek and I were running the Boston chapter of the Industrial Designers Society of America. I know we were seeing the same signals in the Boston design community—we talked about it a lot. The walls between different design fields were coming down. Designers had organized themselves by their unique discipline, architects connecting with architects, graphic designers with graphic designers, industrial designers with industrial designers, and so on.

But something was changing. Designers were realizing they had more in common regardless of field, and that, at the end of the day, all designers generate experiences—it's just a matter of how those experiences manifest. There was more to learn from each other across disciplines. Derek and I realized the most interesting content was at the intersections between disciplines and that cross-pollination could be very valuable to the broader design community.

Elements of the civic and design community started moving in that direction. Then-Governor of Massachusetts Deval Patrick hired the first-in-the-nation Creative Economy Director—basically, a cross-pollinator to boost the creative economy. The first person to serve in the role was Jason Schupbach, a unique design leader and community builder. Jason was absolutely key in getting Design Museum Boston off the ground, but more on that later.

One of the first projects Jason supported was the Design Industry Group of Massachusetts, also known as DIGMA. The group was made up of design industry leaders in Massachusetts looking to elevate the design industry in the Commonwealth. As the chapter chairs of IDSA Boston, Derek and I met DIGMA's first director, Beate Becker, and learned about their mission and approach. A wave was clearly building in the Boston design community.

The idea for a Boston design museum was still ricocheting around my brain. This could be the moment for it, and I didn't want to miss it. It was the conditions in the market that ultimately spurred me to psych myself up enough to mention the idea to Derek. When I did, it was as natural as any other conversation we've ever had in our long friendship. In the middle of a conversation about what we should work on next, I just said, "We should start a design museum." And he replied, "We should!"

————

Derek being so into the idea of starting a design museum in Boston gave me a gigantic rush of confidence. I wasn't crazy! There was something here, and now there were two people who believed in it. I finally had someone to openly discuss the idea with and someone who would build this with me. I had a co-founder. If I hadn't spoken up to Derek, the Design Museum idea may have just rattled in my mind for another few years, never to be made real. Derek and I met regularly to talk about teaching and our IDSA Boston chapter plans, but now our focus was on shaping Design Museum Boston. We talked about it constantly. Seeing his ideas and my ideas blend and shape the vision was incredible. And Derek wanted to share our vision with folks we could trust to get some early feedback and advice.

Derek spent four years studying industrial design under the department chair at MassArt, James (Jamie) Read, and at the time, I worked for Jamie, teaching industrial design as an adjunct professor at night while working full-time at Bose. Jamie was someone we trusted. He was part of the design industry as both a practitioner and educator. So we set up some time and met in Jamie's little office on the tenth floor of the MassArt tower.

We ordered pizza and got right to it. We had an idea to start a new museum in Boston, focused on design—we were going to start trying to raise money, find a space, and make it

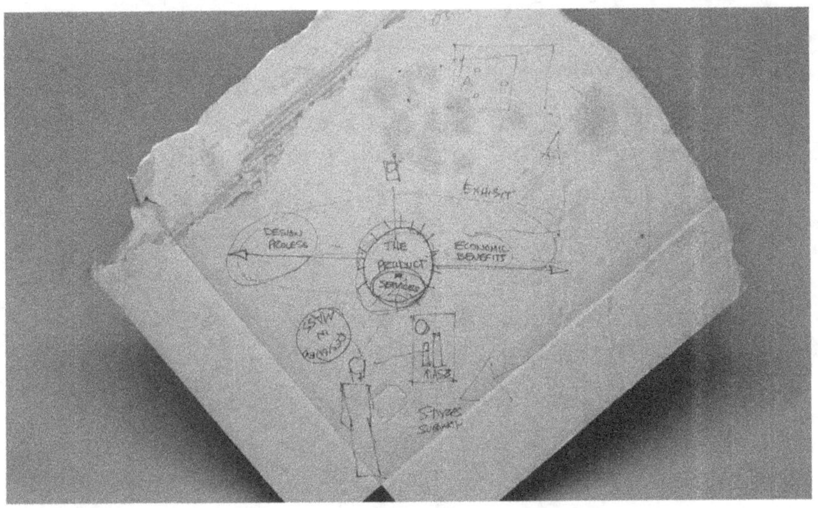

The pizza box where we sketched our initial ideas for public design programs.

happen. We asked Jamie what he thought. His first reaction? He thought we were nuts. Derek and I were 26 years old at this meeting. We already had good, solid jobs. Why would we want to do this? We explained the reasons and ideas behind our vision for Design Museum Boston, and Jamie's protective facade began to crack. He liked the idea; he was just worried about us—he knew this was a huge undertaking for anyone. Derek and I could both see the spark in him as he told us about an old exhibition idea he and others developed that celebrated the design work coming out of the Commonwealth of Massachusetts. They called the exhibit "Design Massachusetts." It showed how so many of the products we use every day are envisioned and designed right in Massachusetts, without many people even realizing it.

I seized on this past program. What if we could make this exhibition happen, and not just install it once, but travel it around the commonwealth? We had long since finished the pizza, so I grabbed the box, tore off the lid, flipped it over, and started sketching the vision for what Design Museum Boston could be: a place for exhibitions and events that showed people all the creativity, strategy, art, and intelligence that go into designing everything they see, touch, and experience, from buildings to furniture, products to signage, website, apps, everything.

At the center of the mental model were the designs that we see and interact with daily. To the left was the design process that leads to what we see and know. To the right was the impact the design has on people, businesses, and the environment. And why stop at just one exhibition? In creating a design museum, we could elevate design, bring it to the public, and inspire more awareness in people to demand better design from designers. It was all there on the back of that pizza box—in fact, it still is. I still have the pizza box with that sketch, grease stains and all.

The next evening, we were across the street from MassArt at Wentworth Institute of Technology, where I also taught industrial design. We shared our vision with my boss and the head of the industrial design department there, Sam Montague. Sam was thrilled by the idea and so supportive. He agreed instantly that Boston needed a design museum, and he helped Derek and me feel so confident that we were just the two people to pull it off.

A few days later, Derek came by my apartment to make it all official. We planned to use Legalzoom.com to formally incorporate the business and we each put up $500 of our money to get things going. We sat at my little desk in front of my computer and went through the online prompts, put in my credit card information, and then we paused before hitting the submit button. We agreed that if we were going to do this together, we should click *Submit* together. Together, we clicked the mouse button at the same time to submit the legal paperwork.

———

Derek and I have similar backstories. We both came from big Italian-American families focused on caring for each other and others. We are both the oldest sibling, and we both had entrepreneurial role models in our parents. Derek watched and then helped run the family pharmacy; I observed and then participated in my parents' side gig of designing, making, and selling seasonal decorations and home decor at local craft shows and fairs.

Derek and I were both industrial designers working in corporations—me at Bose designing speakers and consumer electronics, and Derek at Philips designing commercial lighting, and then Staples working on office supplies and furniture. Derek and I both found design as our calling in life. We also complemented each other. I was very concerned about getting things right. I was clever but more comfortable planning than executing. Derek was fearless and would rather things be good and done than perfect and not. He could also convince anyone of anything. We were similar, but we were two different people with similar but different visions for what Design Museum Boston could be.

When you have multiple people with multiple visions for something, the best thing you can do is get everything out of your heads and onto paper. Derek and I aligned our ideas by creating a simple vision statement—an eight-page booklet describing the who, what, why, and how behind our vision for Design Museum Boston. Putting things on paper makes them real. Plus, once you have things down on paper, you have an

artifact you can share with people to pitch the idea. We went
for an official-looking document so we could use the booklet to
convince others to support us, join our cause, or fund our
venture. The cover showed the preliminary logo I designed,
and there was a title page with our contact info and a table of
contents that served as more of a teaser that went something
like this:

Who we are.

What we want to do.

Why do this?

How we're going to do it.

Pretty straightforward, right? The first page was simple: photos
of Derek and me, and our bios, outlining who we were and
playing up the fact that we were exactly the two guys to launch
this museum. Below our individual bios, we had a combined
bio that showed what we had accomplished together. The
second page had an image of bricks. Why? We wanted to
cement in people's minds that we were going to be a real,
brick-and-mortar museum. The photo of bricks symbolized
our aspiration to have a building. This was the "what." We
wanted to create a physical hub for design education in
Boston.

The next spread of pages was the "why," with a big map
of New England and a photo of the Boston skyline. We cited
some of the Design Industry Group of Massachusetts's
(DIGMA) data. Through their research, they estimated that
over 44,500 people were employed in design in Massachusetts
alone. We thought that since Boston is the unofficial capital or
"hub" of New England, our museum could have an impact
beyond just Boston and Massachusetts. We wanted to serve the
whole New England region.

We wanted to show everyone the power of the design process to make an impact. We did want to be a hub for all designers, no matter what field they practiced in, but more importantly, we believed that since design impacts everyone, the Design Museum should be for everyone. It should be accessible to folks who want to learn more. You don't need to be a scientist to visit a science museum. We wanted to create a design museum where you didn't need to be a designer to visit, learn, and enjoy.

Next in our vision statement booklet was the "how." We had a page with a Gantt chart-style schedule showing when we would launch our web presence and initial exhibition, and when we would officially open the museum. We included very vague and forgiving dates because we wanted to give ourselves a lot of wiggle room to do what we said we were going to do. A key part of this schedule was to produce an initial exhibition before the actual opening of the museum—we envisioned partnering with an existing organization (we didn't know who) to create a proof of concept that would allow us to more effectively fundraise for the physical space we planned to open. The idea was to show funders our vision in real life and give them a taste of what Design Museum Boston could be. The schedule was simple yet official-looking—launch on the web, launch a proof of concept in someone else's space, then launch the actual museum.

The next two pages are my favorite because we included a cleaner illustration of that sketch I drew on the back of the pizza box in Jamie Read's office at MassArt. The graphic showed our curatorial approach. In the middle was the designed artifact, a product, graphic, building, website, etc. To the left we showed the creative process that led to that artifact, and to the right of the artifact was the impact of that design on society, economy, and the environment. Attached to this illustration was information on how our audience would engage in this framework. Starting from the left and the design process, we needed designers to partner with us to share their design work with the museum and our audience. In doing so, we would build a community of designers eager to engage with us and our broader community. The general public would learn so much by seeing the entire design process, valuing the well-designed artifact, and understanding the impact behind all the design they see, use, and experience every day.

The very last page probably should have been the first. It had photos of design museums around the world. There were design museums in various major cities, so why not Boston? We got twenty copies of our vision statement printed and spiral bound. We felt very official holding these booklets. It felt like our idea was real and that the two of us were aligned on what we were moving forward to create together. Then we caught all the spelling mistakes. We fixed them, got another twenty copies printed, and then we were ready to start sharing our vision with more people.

———

Derek was very well-connected at Massachusetts College of Art and Design. He served in student government, and he knew just about everyone from the president all the way to the janitors on each floor of the tower building. During our meeting with Jamie Read, Derek and Jamie came to the same idea for our next step: we should pitch our vision for Design Museum Boston to MassArt's president, Kay Sloan. Derek knew her well, and Jaime knew Kay was interested in projects that elevated the creative industries in Massachusetts. In fact,

MassArt was sponsoring and incubating DIGMA at the time. If we could convince Kay that Boston needed a Design Museum, she could make the connections to help us make it happen. Derek and Jamie reached out to the president's office and we booked a meeting.

Things started happening very fast. Before our meeting with Kay, Derek and I received an invite from DIGMA. They were gathering a select group of design leaders to talk and brainstorm about how they could achieve their mission of elevating the design industry in Massachusetts. It was a working session with representatives from the major design firms, government officials, educators, and leaders of the local design professional organizations. As chairs of the Industrial Designers Society of America Boston chapter, Derek and I were on the list.

The meeting took place at Microsoft's New England Research & Development Center (known as Microsoft NERD), and it started off with a networking reception where Derek and I tried to meet as many people as we possibly could. As two twenty-something designers, we were by far the youngest people there, and a lot of people simply ignored us or brushed us off as not important to meet, but we kept on introducing ourselves and chatting with whoever would engage with us. It was at this very event that we first met Jason Schupbach, the state's new Creative Economy Director, as well as a handful of other folks who would become instrumental in the success of the museum.

There was a speaking program led by David Hacin, a prominent architect in Boston, and we heard from Jason's boss, the Director of Economic Development for the Commonwealth of Massachusetts, Greg Bialecki. They each spoke on the importance of the design sector to the overall state economy, and they shared their vision for bolstering the sector much like the state had done with life sciences—which had become a major economic driver in the region because of public and private investment.

It was incredibly inspiring to hear these leaders talk about design. This was 2009—Lehman Brothers imploded in September 2008, and we were still in the throes of the Great Recession, the worst economic disaster since the Great Depression. Economists and government officials were trying to figure out how to jump-start the economy, and DIGMA was an effort to organize leaders within the creative sector to make design a key part of the state's economic recovery strategy.

After the speaking program, it was time for the working session, which the DIGMA team structured sort of like an open mic night. The chairs were all brought in a circle, and anyone could grab the mic and share an idea. There was an awkward silence and much looking around the room as folks wondered who, if anyone, would go first. To my surprise, Derek jumped up immediately and grabbed the mic before anyone else. I started sweating—we hadn't discussed this at all. It wasn't part of our plan. But Derek knew how to seize a moment, and he wasn't afraid to speak about anything in front of anyone. He said, "Hi, I'm Derek Cascio, and I'm here with Sam Aquillano. We have an idea to start a design museum in Boston." I think the audience was just as shocked as I was.

I could read everyone's faces in those first few seconds. Their looks said something like, "Who the hell are these guys?" Derek continued to share elements of our vision, how the best way to elevate design in Massachusetts was to have a place where it could be viewed, talked about, and celebrated—a museum. Boston was such a museum town, and it was time

Derek Cascio and I speaking at the DIGMA gathering at Microsoft in Cambridge, 2009.

to add a design museum to the mix. Then he did something that surprised me even more. He handed the mic to me.

I barely remember what I said, I was so nervous in front of that audience—I had only shared my idea with three people at that point. Derek handed me the mic in front of dozens. As I spoke, I thought about how days ago we had printed our vision statement, and here we were talking to folks from the governor's office and the leading designers in Boston. I spoke about the importance of connecting with the public to broaden the design conversation, and what better way to do that than a museum? In my mind, the overall design community needed something to rally around, and a design museum could be that thing. I sat down and gave Derek a low-key first bump to thank him for creating that opportunity for us.

A few more people spoke up with ideas to support DIGMA's mission, and afterward, networking was a lot easier for us. People came right up to Derek and me with questions about the Design Museum and even asked how to get involved. What started as an idea was now publicly shared, and folks were intrigued. Looking back on that event, many of the volunteers, donors, and even a few board members who engaged with us over the following thirteen years were present at that meeting at Microsoft. Our board member Tracy Swyst was at the event and always says, "I was there for the beginning."

Just a few days after the DIGMA event at Microsoft, Derek and I were back at MassArt. This time, instead of Jamie's cramped office in the design department, we were in the office of the president. Kay Sloan is a quietly sophisticated woman with an air of kindness. Meeting her for the first time, I instantly felt at ease and that she was someone who cared. She cared about everything—art, the college, the faculty, the students, the creative community, the neighborhood, the city— and she believed that creativity could solve problems and make people's lives better. Lucky for us, Kay was at the DIGMA meeting at Microsoft and heard our pitch, so we weren't starting from scratch. After the initial meeting pleasantries and small talk, she wanted to get down to it; she wanted to know how she could help make Design Museum Boston happen. And that's when things really started happening quickly.

———————

There is something so powerful and reassuring about having a co-founder. All of a sudden, you're not alone. Beyond Derek and me having each other's backs and complementing each other's skillsets, there was something else. When we initially shared the idea of starting a design museum, first with Jamie and Sam M., then out loud at the DIGMA event, then with

Kay Sloane, we were together. As one of us spoke, the other nodded along and agreed with everything the other person was saying—the person we were talking to would almost be hypnotized into agreeing as well—because who wants to be the one person out of three that isn't getting it? In the days and weeks ahead, when I shared the idea of the museum with someone one-on-one, with no co-founder at my side, I found this hypnotic power was gone.

Psychologists call this sort of social influence *conformity:* the tendency for people to align their attitudes, beliefs, and behaviors with those of people around them.[1] In the 1930s, social psychologist Muzafer Sherif used a lighting trick called the autokinetic effort to show how people tend to make decisions because they think others might know something they don't. He projected a single, stationary point of light in a dark room. Because of the way our eyes work (or don't work), the light appears to be moving, even though, in reality, it's not. Sherif discovered that participants' judgment of how much the light moved was easily swayed by the judgments of others.[2]

Social psychologist Solomon Asch took this a step further with his experiments in the 1950s. He gathered a group of eight participants for what he called a vision test—to compare the length of various lines. They'd be presented with a line and then a series of other lines, the idea was to choose the line that most matched the original line in length—and the answer was always obvious. Here's the catch: seven of the eight participants were plants who gave the wrong answer on

---

[1] "Conformity," Psychology Today, https://www.psychologytoday.com/us/basics/conformity.

[2] Frank T. McAndrew Ph.D., "The Eternal Challenge of Conformity Pressure," Psychology Today, June 8, 2020, https://www.psychologytoday.com/us/blog/out-the-ooze/202006/the-eternal-challenge-conformity-pressure/.

purpose to see if the eighth participant would conform. On average, about 32% of participants conformed, and over a dozen trials, about 75% of participants conformed at least once, even though they knew the group's answer was wrong.[3] You can put this social influence to work for yourself. A co-founder (or co-founders) adds instant credibility in meetings and pitches because they're already convinced—they're in agreement—which makes it easier to convince others together.

———

You have your idea, you've visualized it for yourself, and in the process, you've convinced yourself to share your idea with some trusted folks—but how do you actually find a co-founder? The best thing you can do is cultivate a big network before you're even looking for a partner. Finding a co-founder (or co-founders) is a lot like trying to fall in love. Some say the harder you try, the harder it is to find love. When you stop looking, it's less hard, and sometimes love finds you. Build your network to increase your chances. Get involved with communities related to your interests. Better yet, volunteer, and do side projects with others. I got involved with IDSA, a professional organization aimed at supporting industrial design professionals. I planned events, set up mentoring opportunities for young designers, and represented the field in Boston. Not only did attendees at our events get to see me do opening remarks and identified me as one of the leaders of the community, but I was also able to meet the thought leaders in our community and beyond and add them to my network.

———

3 Saul Mcleod, Ph.D., "Solomon Asch Conformity Line Experiment Study," Simply Psychology, October 24, 2023, https://www.simplypsychology.org/asch-conformity.html/.

You don't need to lead whatever group or communities you engage with, but I recommend you engage—in person, if possible. It's about making organic, meaningful connections. These days, tools like LinkedIn and Discord make it easier than ever to maintain a strong network, but it's hard to replace the relationships you build in person. One of our board members at the Design Museum, Scott Englander, met his co-founder by attending Design Museum Boston events. Scott and Jay met at one of our gatherings, and as they kept seeing each other at various museum events, they continued to talk about their ideas for sustainable transportation. Then they started a company together. It happens—as long as you engage with other people in real time.

Sam Altman, co-founder of the startup accelerator Y-Combinator is an outspoken proponent of co-founders. He once said, "If you're not in college, and you don't know a co-founder, the next best thing I think is to go work at an interesting company." He implies that college is a great place to build a community and network of strong relationships that can often lead to co-founders finding each other. Derek and I met in college. Whatever it is—college, a company, church, a book club, a professional organization—figure out how you best engage and build relationships.

One of our first, and biggest, supporters, Richard Banfield, has a relationship-building methodology based on how he can help other people. Richard started and ran a design firm called Fresh Tilled Soil and once told me the firm did very little in the way of business development. Instead, he and the team would look at their combined networks and go down the list, brainstorming how they could help people, and then they'd help them. Word gets around, and people remember the folks that remember them—this strategy yielded connections for Richard, Fresh Tilled Soil, and ultimately, clients.

Figure out your approach to connecting with people, and lean into it. Maybe it's about doing side projects with people you like to work alongside. Whatever it is, it's going to create the conditions for potentially finding a co-founder in the future. And even if potential co-founders aren't currently in your network, having a big network will increase your chances that someone in your network knows the perfect person you should meet to build your creative startup. Ideally, you want someone who complements your skillset. Derek and I had a lot of overlapping skills that helped us effectively split the workload, but we also had our specialties.

Derek was so good at talking to people and pitching the museum that he would do it seemingly off the cuff. Pitching with him over the years made me better at sales. I was the planner, focused on strategy and helping us make the right decisions. Derek was action-based. If we needed a particular tool to build an exhibition element, he would immediately drop what he was doing, go buy the tool, and come right back so we could keep going. He never stopped. I was a project manager, making sure everything was moving in the right direction, on schedule, and within budget. The key for us was staying in close communication, so we were always as aligned as possible. What skills do you have? What skills do you need to start and grow your business? Write these in two columns on a page, and refer back to it during and after your co-founder search.

What if you don't have a big network, and you need a co-founder right away? Don't let it stop you from moving forward. Prototype part of your business to get started. If you want to open a cupcake shop, prototype by selling cupcakes online with delivery within a driveable radius of your kitchen. If you want to start an organization that teaches art to kids, partner with the local children's museum, and bring your classes to where kids already go.

Prototyping something and putting it out into the world is going to show folks—including potential co-founders—that you're serious about your venture. The folks you do know and whom you meet will start asking how they can help. Then refer to your two columns of skillsets, yours and the ones you need. Prototyping your business will help you determine what skills you need in a co-founder with more specificity, with the added bonus that people will start coming to you.

That happened to Derek and me as well. There were more people involved in getting the Design Museum off the ground than merely Derek and myself. As we started working on the museum in the early days, we had a ton of help from my brother Steve and Derek's then-girlfriend, (now wife) Jenna Casey. Steve is a web and new media expert. He and I collaborated on businesses as kids, so this was a natural extension. Steve is a brilliant web developer and general problem solver—if a problem can be addressed with technology, he's going to find the solution. He volunteered to lead our efforts to launch a substantial web presence very quickly. He made it possible for us to build a large community within weeks of launching the business.

Jenna Casey was a design organization's ideal volunteer—she is an adept and multi-talented person who can handle graphic design, marketing, event planning, community building, fundraising, customer service, and much, much more. She believes in community at her core. She was so ideal, she was actually our first paid employee—Derek and I hired her as a contractor before we even hired ourselves full-time. But

Early volunteers in a strategy session. From left to right: me, Charles Crawford, Gena Peditto, Derek Cascio, Jenna Casey, Michael DiTullo, and my brother Steve on Skype.

before that, she and Steve were supporting the launch of the Design Museum because they believed in the mission of the museum and it was an exciting way for them to stretch their own skills and expertise.

One of my biggest regrets is that we didn't recognize Steve and Jenna as co-founders from the beginning. The same holds true for the other early volunteers as well: Mary Fichtner who helped with fundraising; Gena Peditto, who helped with marketing and nonprofit operations; Anna Engstrom, who did project management; many others who helped with a myriad of things. These were people who came to us because they saw something in our leadership and in the idea of the museum— they were involved from the beginning when it was just a kernel of an idea in a vision booklet. I knew Anna before starting the museum, but Mary and Gena were new connections who sought us out after learning about the idea of Design Museum Boston. Derek and I would meet this ragtag team of volunteers every week, sometimes twice a week via

Skype from 6-11 pm. We were all in it to win it, together. This was our founding team.

We even had someone tell us she wanted to be the third founder. A few days after our public launch party in March 2010, a talented design strategist, one of my design students from Wentworth Institute of Technology, Adrianne Harrington, met with Derek and me and had the courage to say she wanted to be the third member of this founding team. We politely dismissed the idea. Years later, I would still ask myself, *What if we had recognized and elevated these folks back then? Where would the design museum be now?* Derek and I had slipped into a false startup archetype described as "the hero's journey." It's a social construct that favors a particular kind of story, one where the singular hero takes the path to save the day. Think Luke Skywalker taking on the empire, Neo saving Zion from the machines, or Spiderman defeating Green Goblin. Most founder stories tend to align with this myth and polish over the fact that every founder has help.

Sara Hartmann sits on the Design Museum Everywhere Council and wrote an article for Design Museum Magazine where she stated that if we want to elevate more entrepreneurs, we need to tell the honest stories behind startups—which is what I'm attempting to do here. She advocates for a new kind of startup founding story, one aligned with teams like Ocean's Eleven, or in my opinion, the Avengers, where a group of extraordinary individuals come together to accomplish something big. And that's the real story behind Design Museum. There are potential co-founders around you right now—siblings, friends, co-workers, supporters, volunteers—it's up to you to recognize and elevate them. Let others share in the dream and you'll go far together.

Once you have your co-founder(s), take the time to be clear about who is doing what, even if you're each responsible for a lot. What are your roles and responsibilities? What are your titles? Who "owns" which parts of the business? It may seem extremely presumptuous to define these things so early, but clarity, even clarity that comes from a few awkward conversations, is going to serve you and your business so well. Document this clarity, along with the who, what, why, how, and when of your vision in a document—get it out of your head and onto paper. Make a vision statement. The mere act of creating it together will help align you going forward. Start with who you are, the founders or founding team, your photos, roles, and bios. Then try to create a group bio of who you are as a team. State what you're doing, and describe it in enough detail to be complete, but not so much that your reader loses interest. Try to stay away from future tense verbs like, "We will start a cupcake shop." Instead write, "We're starting a cupcake shop called For Cupcake's Sake." Action matters to people.

Then write about the"why." Maybe your grandfather ran a bakery. Maybe during the COVID-19 lockdowns, you made cupcakes and delivered them to friends and family, and they loved them. Cupcakes make people happy and you want to spread that happiness. In the case of our youth arts example, maybe art was instrumental in defining your childhood and opening up new opportunities, and you want to do that for other kids. Share your "why" by being vulnerable and bringing people inside your mind and along for your adventure. Finally, share the how and the when. Be as specific as you can without locking yourself into a plan you can't achieve because you want to show people that you can make a plan and execute it. This vision statement will not only align the founding team, but you can also use it to pitch your business to partners, investors, and customers—take the time to make this foundational document.

CHAPTER 3

Build a Community from Day One

Every business needs one.

"Alone, we can do so little; together, we can do so much."
— Helen Keller

Starting a venture alone is not setting yourself up for success. You need someone, or a group of people, who is 100% with you. My brother and I created a successful landscaping business in our teens because we had each other. Don, Ori, and I created the Thought at Work conference together, and with a huge team of volunteers at RIT, many of them juniors and sophomores who continued to create Thought at Work for years to come. When Derek grabbed the microphone at the DIGMA event, he altered the course of our journey and accelerated our debut—something I never would have done alone. The Design Museum wouldn't exist without Derek, Jenna, Steve, Mary, Gena, Anna, and our community— together, we are the heroes of this story.

I grew up within a supportive environment of many nested communities. As a child in a large, extended Italian-American family, I was constantly surrounded by grandparents, aunts, uncles, and cousins. We had community leaders, namely my Grandma Connie and her three daughters, Pam, Wendy (my mother), and Kelly. Together, these four incredible women created one of the tightest, most supportive communities I've ever seen or experienced in my life. It is a group of people that is always there for each other, no matter what. If you needed something, someone would be there; if you needed to talk, someone would listen. This didn't just happen—although, as a child, it seemed effortless—my grandmother, mom, and aunts deliberately built and maintained this community, and they still do every day.

Every community has forums to connect and engage with other members. There are rituals, which are activities you can always count on happening, as well as artifacts that define the group's shared experience. My big Italian family was no different. Our forums were the welcoming homes that each of these women designed and maintained as safe, comfortable spaces for gathering. Our rituals included a weekly Sunday pasta dinner at my grandparent's house with the entire extended family. We celebrated every single cousin's birthday together with a big family party—and for holidays like Easter, Independence Day, Thanksgiving, and Christmas, we were always together. And there were the artifacts that surrounded these forums and rituals: the pots, pans, and dishes for the pasta dinner; the long extended table we all sat around; the toys we played with. Throughout my life, this community supported me when I needed it the most. They made me feel special and seen and defined who I am.

Your startup needs the same thing to survive and thrive. You need a community of fans and supporters to lift your venture out of obscurity and make it successful. It's up to you to deliberately and intentionally design the conditions for your community to exist and cultivate it over time.

Derek and I recruited an amazing team of volunteers to support the launch of Design Museum Boston. The very next thing we did was create a community around our nascent museum. Why was that our next step? Why didn't we snap into fundraising mode or start creating exhibitions? Derek and I both believe that design is for everyone—design impacts all of us every day in so many ways, but so few people know what design is or what designers do. At the core of our vision for the Design Museum was making design more accessible. We wanted to demystify and democratize design so that people would understand it better and demand good design that could make life better.

We were kind of obsessed with transparency—too often, the design process is invisible to the people we're designing for. We wanted to change that. This belief in accessibility manifested in every aspect of growing our startup. We decided to make the establishment of the museum an accessible process and develop the museum idea in full view of the public. From the start, we worked to create an open forum for communication, to hear directly from our potential audience about what they wanted and needed from a design museum.

With my brother Steve's help, we started with a simple landing page on designmuseumboston.org, stating our active intention to establish a new design museum in Boston. We had no money and a one-page website, but that page made us real. We knew we were going to need as much help as we could get, and we found very early that people wanted to do more than make a small donation or write a check. They wanted to be involved. They wanted community.

Successful communities create a sense of belonging, that human need to feel connected and accepted by others. Belonging provides a sense of security, purpose, and identity. Done well, a brand community can create that necessary space for people, as well as drive long-term loyalty and revenue growth. IBM and Ipsos collaborated on a study that found top brands that focused on community and belonging grew their revenue at three times the rate of lower-performing brands over six years, and saw market share gains upwards of ten percent higher.[4] This is powerful stuff for your fledgling creative startup.

We harnessed the power of community by quickly launching designingamuseum.org in late October 2009, just ahead of the DIGMA meeting at Microsoft (the one where Derek swiped the open mic). Designingamuseum.org was an online community where folks could become members and contribute their thoughts, ideas, and feedback. Words matter. So we boldly stated that we didn't have everything figured out and that we needed help. We were inviting people to join our team—they could be part of bringing a new museum to life.

To our amazement, people started becoming members. Within just a few days, we had 500 members on designingamuseum.org, and folks were sharing words of encouragement for Derek, me, and the team. They loved the idea of starting a design museum in Boston—many wondered in their posts why this hadn't happened before, as it seemed so needed. All of a sudden we had hundreds of people we could

---

[4] Mercedes Cardona, "Alone or Together, IBM Study Says 'Brand Belonging' Pays Off," Velocitize, November 20, 2017, https://velocitize.com/2017/11/20/alone-or-together-ibm-study-says-brand-belonging-pays-off/.

ask for advice. In many ways, it was kind of liberating. We didn't need to have all the answers ourselves. We had access to the ultimate think tank for our startup: our future audience.

We created the ritual of regularly asking our community for their ideas and advice. It didn't just happen. We deliberately opened the door for their involvement. We made it clear not every idea had to come from Derek or me or the founding volunteers—ideas could come from anywhere. We just had to be open to hearing from folks and acknowledge their contributions. This approach to accessibility and transparency worked so well that we enshrined it in our core values. This would be how we would run the museum forever.

The artifacts of our community at this point were digital —people's posts, ideas, and links to other organizations we could learn from—it was a treasure trove of community artifacts, all usable in our quest to start a new museum. Within weeks, the community grew to over 1,000 members on the site, with ongoing posts and conversations. The dialogue and connections started transitioning over into the real world.

If there's something I don't know how to do, I get a book (or books) and read about it—it's my go-to first step for any kind of learning. So naturally, to understand how to start a nonprofit, I read a book on how to start a new nonprofit. I learned that every nonprofit in the United States is required by law to have a board of directors, and the founder(s) have the responsibility of appointing the first board members who would then oversee and advise on the work of the organization. In my mind, a Board of Directors would form the second concentric circle of nesting communities around our team, closely supporting our work. I didn't need to look too far to build this important core community of board members. We had over 1,000 people already engaged in our idea.

I got a sheet of paper and made two columns: one for the qualities I wanted in a board member, and one for the characteristics I wanted to avoid. I wanted to recruit founding board members who were passionate about the idea, innovative thinkers, and entrepreneurs. I wanted folks who had a bit more experience than Derek and me, but not so much experience that they would balk at some of our more unique ideas for what a museum could be and how we wanted to operate. I took that list of characteristics to Derek, and we started looking at our personal and professional networks, as well as our community members—it was time to ask some folks to join as board members, the most engaged volunteers yet.

Michael DiTullo was really active on designingamuseum.org, sharing ideas and encouraging us to keep going. Michael is an extremely talented and smart designer who has made a name for himself working on sneakers for Michael Jordan and other professional athletes, as well as designing lots of other products, vehicles, branding, and experiences for well-known brands. Most industrial designers also know Michael because he is so generous with his time by speaking at events, giving sketching demos, and mentoring the next generation of designers. Back then, I saw Michael as an innovator who would help us connect the museum to a global network of designers very quickly. I reached out with a private message on designingamuseum.org and asked if I could buy him dinner.

We met at a trendy restaurant in Cambridge, Massachusetts. I was still getting used to talking to people about the Design Museum. Michael has always been a generously curious person—he wanted to hear all about where the idea came from, what we were working on, and how he could help. At times in the conversation, I felt like I was making things up on the fly—it was all still so new—but I had the image of our vision statement in my mind: we wanted to make design more accessible to the public by uniting designers of all stripes to share their creative work in transparent, interesting, and fun ways that people could easily connect with. That was music to Michael's ears. He wanted more people to know about and understand design because he believed it could make the world a better place. In fact, he compared design directly to music during our conversation.

Most people enjoy some kind of music, they know of musicians, and maybe they've even seen them perform. Seeing a musician perform gives you more understanding and respect for their craft, deepening your relationship with the creative output and creating a desire for more good music. Michael posited, "What if we could do that for design? What if people had favorite designers and understood the creative process? What if they demanded good design from designers because they understand the creative process and the impact of good design?"

It struck me that this was exactly what we were hoping to accomplish with Design Museum Boston. On the spot, I asked Michael if he would join our board of directors and help us make that vision a reality. I think I caught him off guard—he was surprised but intrigued. He asked what it meant to be on the board (he had never joined a board before). In truth, I had just learned what a board was supposed to do for a nonprofit, but of course, I spoke with confidence, as if I knew exactly what I was talking about. I was selling this after all.

I let Michael know that the board would oversee Derek's and my work, help us make connections and fundraise, give generously of both time and money, and generally be an ambassador and evangelist for this new institution. Michael was very into it and asked who else was on the board. "Well," I replied, "you're the first person I've asked. Perhaps we can grow the board together." I was right about Michael's entrepreneurial spirit. He told me he had to talk to his wife Kristina about it, and he'd let me know as soon as possible. A few days later, he called me and let me know he was officially in—our first board member. And he already had ideas for who else we could recruit. Our core community was growing.

We continued to grow the board, next adding Jordan Nollman. Jordan is a friend of Michael's, Derek's, and mine who has worked for some of the top design firms in the U.S. and started his own design firm called Sprout. Jordan is an innovator and an entrepreneur, check and check. Then we added Ted Acworth, who would chair our founding board— we first met Ted at the DIGMA meeting at Microsoft. He developed the technology for and founded a company called Artaic, which used specialized software and a robot to make tile mosaics for interior architecture from any digital photo.

Then Robert Reimann joined, a leader in the user experience design space who co-wrote the undisputed bible on user interface design. I was fortunate to work directly with Robert at Bose and consider him a mentor and friend. Then Michael connected us to Dan Borelli who led exhibition design at the Harvard Graduate School of Design. These five friends made up our first board, and over the subsequent years, we grew our board into a group of people representative of our community, including people of different genders, members of color, and folks who brought their unique life experiences to our collective work. Our board would become our core community of support, with most of our successes connected to, or traceable back to, someone from our Board of Directors.

―――――

The weekly spaghetti dinners at my grandparents' were a ritual for my family community—an event we could always count on to all be together. I loved planning events. I enjoy all the preparation and experience design ahead of the actual moment. I thrive in the planning stage, putting myself in the shoes of my attendees and imagining what they will experience when they arrive. Then there's the thrill of the moment when all your preparation comes together, and there's very little you can do. It's happening, and you're along for the ride. Seeing the reactions and smiles on attendees' faces, hearing their feedback on a great experience—I get such a high from a well-executed event.

I planned events as a kid, in high school (we called them parties), and in college (guest lectures and the Thought at Work conference I mentioned in chapter two). After college, I continued to bring people together with events in my corporate job. My friends and I felt the need for some outside-of-work team building and created Crushtoberfest, an annual fall gathering coinciding with Halloween and Movember. So yes, our event included a mustache-growing competition, costumes, and (for some reason) feats of strength competitions. With Derek, for the Industrial Designers Society of America, we planned workshops, panel discussions, and more. Derek and I both knew from experience that events would be a major part of our community-building strategy for Design Museum Boston.

We started planning our first event for the Design Museum: our public launch party. The vision was a very public, coming-out event that would gather designers from all over Boston and introduce them to this big idea, while hopefully raising some money to support our growth. Ever ambitious, we also planned to launch our main website, designmuseumboston.org, that same night. The date was set for March 16, 2010—well into the new year, with enough time to plan and market the event to our audience. Plus, it would be getting a bit warmer in Boston, and people would want to come out. We needed a venue. This was always hard for us because we had no idea how many people would actually show up, plus we had precious little budget for this event—we could not afford to rent a place.

Derek had the idea of using a bar with an underutilized event space. He found West End Johnnie's, a somewhat quirky bar/restaurant filled with Boston sports memorabilia in the first-floor dining area. There were seats from Fenway Park, a Celtics basketball, and much more. The dining area wasn't our scene, but Derek remembered seeing a basement event space that was pretty neat. It was barebones but had a giant gold neon sign that said "NAKED," so that was something—it did give the whole space an orangey tint, which was cool. Besides that weird giant sign, we could make the space into whatever we wanted. Using his Derek magic, he scored us a meeting with West End Johnnie himself, John Caron, the owner of the restaurant. We explained our idea to start a new museum and that we had no money, but we could promise a ton of people at his bar that night. John was interested. He asked, "This is supposed to be a fundraiser for you guys, right?" We nodded. "How about I split the bar tab with you at the end of the night, 50/50?" We shook on it.

We got to work planning the event experience and designing the website. The whole volunteer team was working every evening through the night to prepare. We found a DJ/emcee, our pal Craig Rubino, with whom I went to college, so I knew he could handle a big audience. Through designingamuseum.org, we connected with Brandon Bird, a freelance exhibition designer, and asked him if he would be up for helping us design a small exhibition on the potential for a design museum in Boston—he said yes, and worked on transforming one of the side rooms into a Design Museum branded experience.

We connected with the many design and creative service firms who sponsored our Industrial Designers Society of America (IDSA) events in the past—firms like ELEVEN, Essential, Korn Design, Continuum, and more agreed to sponsor the event with money and silent auction items. We gathered as many computers as we could find, and Steve set up an area where folks could be the first to check out the new website and ask him any questions. And, of course, Derek and I created a digital slideshow and prepared our remarks. We opened up RSVPs for *Prepare to Launch* on designingamuseum.org and made sure everyone in our core community posted and shared as widely as they could. We also reached out to all the professional design chapters in the area, like the IDSA, American Institute of Graphic Arts, American Institute of Architects, Graphic Artists Guild, and more.

RSVPs started rolling in/ This was happening. We were getting the attention of the design community and, thankfully, the press. We received an email from Christopher Muther, a lead arts reporter for the Boston Globe—he wanted to chat about what we were working on, and we were beyond thrilled to get our message out. We chatted with Christopher for a couple of hours, sharing our bios and backstories. We even told him about sketching the idea for the museum on the back of a pizza box at MassArt. He knew we were in the early stages, but Christopher asked where we wanted to go with this idea. A few days later, we were invited to do a photoshoot with Globe photographer Essdras Suarez. He photographed Derek and me walking around Downtown Boston, and our friends Duane Smith and Stefane Barbeau graciously allowed us to use their design store, Vessel, as a makeshift photo studio as well.

To our astonishment, the next Sunday Globe had a full-page photo of Derek and me on the cover of the Arts & Style section. The title was, *Out of the box, How a pair of 27-year-olds are realizing their dream for a traveling museum of local design.* Derek and I grabbed as many copies as we could find and started sharing the Boston.com version of the article online—everyone from our team, board, and community was over the moon. Here it was: solid social proof that we were doing something important and amazing.

Christopher's article began with, "Few museums can trace their beginnings to some hurried sketches made on the back of a pizza box. Then again, few museums have grown from concept to reality as quickly as Design Museum Boston. It began two years ago when Bose Corp. product designer Sam Aquillano and Philips Color Kinetics designer Derek Cascio were discussing ways to boost the profile of the Massachusetts design community. The state is a hotbed of product design, architecture, urban planning, interior design, video game animation, graphic design, and apparel, but Aquillano and Cascio realized that most people outside the design community have no idea that everything from the Swiffer to the video game Rock Band originated here."

Muther also interviewed leaders in the design industry and state government, including Beatte Becker from the Design Industry Group of Massachusetts, Jason Schupbach from the governor's office, and our very own board member, Michael DiTullo. Michael's quote nicely summed up his passion and reason for being involved: "When Sam and Derek decided to donate so much of their free time to this cause, I definitely wanted to become involved. I saw it as a way to get our voice to the public. They don't always have an understanding of everything design impacts. Everything around us in this man-made environment is touched by a designer." The Boston Globe feature boosted RSVPs dramatically for our launch party—Muther had generously mentioned the March 16 fundraising event, with a link to our website at the end of the article. We continued planning and prepping for the event, amazed that hundreds of people were going to celebrate this new museum with us.

The day before the party, we received another press request, this time to be on the Callie Crossley Show on WGBH Radio, one of Boston's NPR stations. So the morning of our launch event started with Derek and me in a little sound studio at WGBH radio, talking about our vision. Of course, we invited everyone listening to join us at West End Johnnie's later that night. I love NPR radio, so this was a dream come true. I left the studio absolutely floating, but then it was back to reality —we had an event to execute.

Luckily, we weren't alone. My mother Wendy and brother Steve flew in to help. My then-girlfriend, now-wife, Nicole, was there as well. Derek's girlfriend and Design Museum super volunteer Jenna Casey was there along with the rest of our volunteer team, board members, and a handful of my students

Volunteers at Prepare for Launch event, March 2010.

from Wentworth Institute of Technology, who volunteered to help prep and work various roles during the event.

We got set and people started arriving—a lot of people. Over 400 people packed into the basement event space at West End Johnnie's, curious to learn about this new museum and asking how they could help. The music was great. Craig was spinning tunes and keeping the crowd engaged with all the activities we had for them. They could demo the new website, check out Brandon's exhibition, bid on the silent auction, and drink and network with others in the community.

Derek and I took every opportunity to talk to all the guests, introducing ourselves and inviting people to join our online community and email newsletter to stay in the know. We talked to everyone from design students and leaders of top design firms to business owners and government officials. What I heard most from folks was an acknowledgment that we were in the middle of one of the worst recessions in history, but there was also a lot of hope and excitement for new ideas like Design Museum Boston, and people were ready to help where and when they could.

Prepare to Launch was our first public event, and it was a huge success. We raised roughly $10,000 from sponsors, donations, and the silent auction. In one night, we multiplied our initial $1,000 investment donation times ten. At the end of the night, after the crowd cleared out, it was just John, Derek, and I left. John was smoking a big cigar, counting a huge pile of cash at the bar with an equally huge smile on his face. "So, was it a success?" he asked, talking with the cigar still mashed between his teeth. We said yes, it definitely was. Then he split the stack, handed it to Derek, and said, " You can party here any time."

Events were pivotal to our community and awareness-building efforts—even those early events mattered. Perhaps they mattered most of all. Thirteen years later, I can still connect dots to connections, donations, and partnerships that originated at the DIGMA meeting, our launch party, or from our online community. And each event led to the next event.

After *Prepare to Launch,* I received an email from Derek Mekita, a studio manager at Office Environments, a furniture and office equipment seller. Derek M. learned about Design Museum Boston from our online community and heard about the launch party—he wanted to connect about building a partnership between Office Environments and the museum. When we met Derek M. and his colleague Meghan Allen at their showroom, Derek C. and I were blown away by the space. It was beautiful, gleaming white with the most gorgeous modern furniture, plus big windows looking out at Boston's Seaport and the harbor.

Meghan explained that for years, Office Environments had been involved with the same design organizations as their competitors, and they were hoping to reach new audiences and customers. They traditionally collaborated with interior designers and organizations focused on interior design, but they wanted to connect with all types of designers and folks outside design, as well. When they heard about our approach of uniting the various design fields and making an accessible organization so that anyone interested in design could participate, they thought, "This is perfect."

Together with Meghan, Derek M., and Office Environments (now called Red Thread), we started our first recurring event series. Our collective goal was to unite people around the idea of starting a new Design Museum, so we called the series *UNITE*. Each event was at a different design location around Greater Boston—for example, this first event was titled *UNITE @ Office Environments*. With this strategy, we could partner with organizations to host the events. They would invite their communities, we would invite ours, and everyone could connect and learn about the Design Museum. What's more, we truly did not have the time nor the capacity to plan event after event—Derek and I were still working full-time. With *UNITE*, the host venue would do most of the planning and production work. We marketed each event and showed up with a big audience.

Meghan and Derek M. knew how to throw a party. The first *UNITE* event took place in July 2010. Once again, hundreds of people gathered to learn about the museum and connect with the growing Design Museum community. We had the beginnings of a forum (even if it did move every time) and a ritual. We united every three months at a new location, and at each event, Derek and I spoke about the museum and

UNITE event at Office Environments, July 2010.

our progress, and we always answered questions. Designers and non-designers alike came to Office Environments and each following *UNITE* event.

Aside from the great food (Derek had built a partnership with Boloco for us to offer burritos at each event), my favorite part of UNITE was recognizing our amazing volunteers. At Office Environments, we brought Jenna Casey, Mary Fichtner, Brandon Bird, and more up on stage. In the crowd were Michael DiTullo, Jordan Nollman, and the rest of our Board of Directors along with Adriane Harrington and other dedicated volunteers. We were bringing people together from every ring of our nested community: team, board, volunteers, and audience. Each event built awareness and drove new meetings and partnerships—the system was working, and we were on a roll.

Any business and organization can and should build a community. Whether it's a group of 10 close advisors or 10,000 members online, your community is an asset that will pay dividends for years to come in terms of opportunities, connections, and\ revenue. For example, my local brewery, True West cultivates community through their *Mug Share* program. You purchase a special ceramic mug for an annual fee, and it gets numbered and personalized on the bottom— that's your mug at the brewery. The mug is extra large, 20 oz., but you only pay for a 16 oz. fill each time, so the extra beer is extra nice. I became a member because I want to support local businesses—and let's be honest, I want to be seen supporting local businesses. True West has a community email newsletter, and they do special events for members to gather and drink their creations. True West uses the money from the *Mug Share* to send their brewing staff to conferences, so I always feel like I'm supporting the very people making good beer for me and my neighbors. And if they have any money from the program left over at the end of the year, they donate it to the local youth sports leagues—who doesn't want to help fund kids playing outside?

For your business, you need to figure out the *why* or *whys* behind people engaging in your community. Each person's *why* might be different, but you can be intentional about creating these. One of the *whys* might simply be you. You are exciting, and people want to be near you because you're doing something cool. I know there were people in our community early on who simply wanted to connect closely with Derek and me, and that was great. Many of those people became true friends of ours over the years. Maybe folks want to connect with others with the same interests and values, be in the know, or have a chance to give back and make a difference. Maybe they just want the special benefits that come from being a member of your community. Brainstorm your community *whys* with your team and write them down, so you can design a community experience around them—then create the *hows* that satisfy the *whys*.

You can also think about your community as nested concentric circles. Your team is in the middle—that's you and your co-founder(s). The next circle out is your core group of supporters. For us, that was our Board of Directors—as a nonprofit, we are required by law to have a board, but any organization or business can have a group of advisors, formal or informal. I highly recommend every entrepreneur at least have a group of advisors they can lean on when they need to.

In fact, at the Design Museum, we now have a Board of Directors and a Council of Advisors who also support the work. From our experience, there are people who have made it in their lives and careers, and they want to give back—when they were just starting out, someone helped them, and they want to pay it forward. There are also folks who want to be entrepreneurs and either feel like they missed their chance (it's never too late) or that it's just not right for them, but they want to engage in entrepreneurship vicariously. And some people just wanted to help us, and they were so generous and amazing —it was simply up to us to ask and then express gratitude.

Think about the gaps in your founding team's skills, and recruit people to be advisors that fill those gaps. Figure out your forums, rituals, and artifacts for each concentric circle of your nested communities, including an advisory group. Our ritual was to have a board meeting every three months. Even if you don't have a board of directors, I recommend at least having a quarterly meeting with your co-founders to step back and analyze where you are and where you need to go. If you want to create an advisory group, think about the community elements that will make being involved with your business special for them, since they're giving up their time (and, hopefully, money) to support you.

But one quick word of caution on advisory groups. While I whole-heartily recommend every business have at least a handful of advisors, please don't think you have to listen and do everything they say—you just need to listen, ask questions, and make them feel special. If one of your advisors gets upset that you don't listen and act on their advice, it's probably time to part ways. If an advisor is only in it to see their will be done, regardless of your thoughts, then it's not the right fit, and you need to be okay with that, too.

The next circle out from the core supporters is your actively engaged community—these are the folks who are very involved. Maybe they're your volunteers or most enthusiastic customers. Treat them as such with special access to forums, rituals, and artifacts. Finally, there is your audience or customer community that wants to be aware of what's going on—maybe they don't engage as much, but they're still affiliated with you and your brand. I recommend designing forums, rituals, and artifacts for all three sub-communities to create a unified customer experience around your brand.

Let's look at two example startups. First our cupcake shop, *For Cupcake's Sake*. Yes, I recommend even a cupcake shop have an advisory group and certainly a community. Perhaps our advisory group is a small group of people that help you think through business issues and solve problems. Maybe your cousin is an expert in social media marketing, and your best friend is an accountant. The forum and ritual could be that every three months, you meet at your favorite restaurant for lunch and spend a solid ninety minutes asking questions and getting advice. The artifact could be giving them coupons for free cupcake deliveries they can send to friends. Bonus, your advisors are now helping to introduce your shop to their friends.

Your next concentric circle of community could be folks in your town or neighborhood who love baking and cupcakes. The forum here is your shop. Perhaps every month, you have a cupcake-tasting event for members, where you can get feedback on your latest ideas. It's a ritual if it happens regularly, and folks can expect and look forward to it. An artifact could be a cupcake passport—your community members get a stamp for each specialty cupcake they taste test. Or perhaps you sell a membership for monthly cupcake-making demos where you invite a small group into your kitchen to learn how to make their own cupcakes. The artifact here is homemade and delicious.

Finally, there's your outermost circle, the general community. Here, I could see your cupcake shop having a vibrant Instagram following and e-mail newsletter with beautiful imagery of your cupcakes and special offers. Maybe here is where you offer a monthly cupcake box subscription. The forum is online, the ritual is getting your box in the mail, and again, the artifacts are delicious and always surprising.

How about a youth arts education nonprofit? Let's call it *Art Scouts*. We'll definitely need a board of directors to be in compliance with the IRS. Develop a simple one-page document with expectations for board members—keeping in mind that most boards for nonprofits are required to make regular donations to their organization. You can find a lot of examples of this online. Think about the skills and expertise you need to succeed. For *Art Scouts*, we'll need experts in arts education, fundraising, marketing, public relations, and more.

Start recruiting! Introduce people to your idea, and ask if they want to serve in support of your mission. The forum for the board might be one of the board member's offices that has a nice conference room where you can all brainstorm and connect. The ritual might be sending the board a summary every quarter of how you're doing financially and how many children you've served. Maybe the artifact is giving board members examples of the kids' creations, so they feel tied to the mission. You meet at the office for the quarterly board meeting then go out to dinner to socialize—this is all supposed to be interesting and fun.

The engaged community for *Art Scouts* gets interesting because there are multiple important constituencies that need your attention. There are the kids, their parents, and likely your donors and supporters, depending on the business model. Each sub-group here likely needs multiple forums, rituals, and artifacts to achieve your mission. Perhaps you offer bi-weekly art classes for kids at the local community center after school, plus multiple sessions on weekends. The forum is the community center, the ritual is your unique art curriculum which celebrates each creation at the end of the session, and the artifacts are the kids' art. Being the *Art Scouts,* maybe the kids get badges for learning certain media and techniques— artifacts! Of course, these communities can overlap. Maybe you plan a parent and donor night twice a year that features an art show, art making for the adults, and an auction to support your mission.

Finally, there's your general audience. In this case, you might want to be off traditional social networks like Facebook since you're working with kids and families. You can create your own online community with photos, at-home art activities, and virtual art demos for kids. Like *For Cupcake's Sake,* maybe you have a subscription box that ships monthly with different art supplies for that month's at-home project. You can tier everything and charge for various opportunities. Across all these nested communities, think about how you move people from your general circle inward to your engaged circle(and even into your advisor circle). Build your fan base deliberately and methodically, and you'll see the benefits in your growth.

It has never been easier to create an online community for your startup. Right now, you can start a Facebook group using your preliminary logo and vision statement. Or launch a Linkedin group—whatever platform makes the most sense for you. There are even more specialized, but still very accessible, tools where you can create your own custom online community—services like Disciple Media, BuddyBoss, and Ning make it possible. All of these platforms have easy-to-use templates and instructions. You're creating channels for communication and ways for folks to engage and participate, which could mean anything from making it easy for people to volunteer or spend money or both. Identify the groups that are naturally going to connect with you and your business, starting with your own personal network and then expanding beyond by utilizing your existing community. Ask people questions, engage them beyond simply selling them something, and make them feel like they're part of your team.

Whatever platform you use online, engage on it regularly —post often, respond to everyone, and where appropriate, try to transition online connections to video conferences or in-person meetings to help build strong relationships. Even better, try to build connections between members—remember Richard Banfield's "How can I help?" strategy? If you can make your community a place where people find joy, camaraderie, answers to their questions, and solutions to their problems, they're going to build a super strong connection to your business for a long, long time.

And then there are events—you guessed it, every business can and should do events. They can be small events for your team and advisors at a local bar, a party for your investors, or a huge gala for your supporters at a hotel ballroom. Events bring people together in space and time, which is so critical for building community. I like to remind people that even a rocket ship business like Instagram did events when it first started. Instagram's founders started by bringing together local photographers in different cities to use the app and give feedback on filters. Now they bring together their amazing network of influencers to drive the kind of content they want to see on the platform.

You should plan a launch party for your business. It doesn't need to happen exactly when you launched—Design Museum Boston was incorporated in August 2009, and our launch party didn't happen until March 2010. But this is a very important milestone to take advantage of. People, and the press, love new things—they're curious. It's called "news" for a reason—you're only new once, and this could be your first and only chance at press attention for a while. Don't miss the opportunity to bring together your early community members and local press, bloggers, social media influencers, and whoever is right for you. I recommend planning a launch party early in your adventure, then creating some kind of regularly recurring event—this could be monthly or quarterly, big or small—and, eventually, add in an annual special event. For our cupcake shop, perhaps that special annual event is a holiday cupcake party; for *Art Scouts*, it's probably an annual fundraising gala. Figure out your community event strategy across your four concentric circles: team, close advisors, engaged community, and audience/customer community.

A community is going to accelerate your business growth for years to come. It's going to help you through the hard times and make the good times that much sweeter. The community we built early on is still paying off. People involved with our work today remember being at the launch party, volunteering at the first *UNITE* event, and sharing their thoughts on designingamuseum.org. We built feelings of accessibility and engagement that persist to this day, underlying and supporting everything we do—we built the Design Museum family. You can do the same. Create a nest of support around you and your founding team. Nurture it and maintain it because it's going to help you innovate, make better decisions, and recover more quickly from mistakes. You do not need to do this alone.

CHAPTER 4

Naysayers Will Say Nay

What will you say?

"At the crossway on the road that leads to the future, each progressive spirit is opposed by a thousand men appointed to guard the past."
— Maurice Maeterlinck, playwright

I'm excited. You're doing it! You have your founding team. You've designed multiple nested communities of support around you and your co-founders. Good on you! At this point, I hate to rain on the parade, but I want you to be ready. I guarantee someone—more like someones—is going to tell you what you're doing is impossible and that you should just stop. It's time to figure out how to handle the naysayers.

Doing the impossible, or what others say can't or shouldn't be done, sort of runs in the family here in the Aquillano household. My wife Nicole fell in love with ceramics as a teen. Working with clay in her high school art class, she came alive as she shaped the material with her bare hands to become something beautiful. She was hooked. She knew exactly what she wanted to do with her life. She held hope for her dream of becoming a studio potter. She wanted to do what she loved for a living. Nicole met resistance. Her parents, teachers, and friends told her it was impossible or not practical or that it would be a mistake—all conjuring up some image of the starving artist. They were worried about her future, and that worry shaped their reactions to her dream.

The worries did their work—at least, for a while. Nicole didn't pursue ceramic arts in college. She attended Carlow University on a full athletic scholarship—she was an amazing softball pitcher—working on a dual degree in mathematics and civil engineering, with coursework at Carnegie Mellon University as well. She kept her dream alive by taking ceramics courses as electives at Carlow. She took those same courses over and over again, honing her craft. Nicole had a mentor at Carlow, Dale Huffman, the head of the ceramics department at the school. When she shared her dream of becoming a studio potter for a living, Dale said, *yes, it's a hard road, but if you work hard enough, anything is possible.*

Nicole graduated, and after a series of civil engineering jobs, she was hired at the Environmental Protection Agency in Boston, MA—an amazing job in her field. At the EPA she tracked companies' wastewater practices and wrote permits to limit their negative environmental impact. She was doing important work, but all the while she was nurturing her real dream of becoming a ceramic artist. After a long day at work, she would attend continuing education courses at Massachusetts College of Art and Design. She didn't need the instruction—she knew how to throw, glaze, and fire—what she needed was access to the wheels, materials, and kilns to continue elevating her art practice. She wasn't just taking continuing education as a hobby. She was building up her portfolio, and she was saving up to go to graduate school.

We visited a handful of MFA programs around Greater Boston, and she applied to even more. To our delight, she was accepted into the prestigious Rhode Island School of Design, where she attended and earned her MFA in ceramics. She ultimately left the EPA to pursue her dream. It was and is a ton of work and a lot of sacrifice, but Nicole is now a successful studio potter going on ten years. She has a home studio where her materials get delivered. She creates tableware like cups, bowls, vases, and more, and UPS, FedEx, and USPS are at our house daily, whisking her work off to people and stores around the world.

It was just recently, after being together almost 15 years, that I found myself in her childhood bedroom looking at pictures and postcards hanging on her bulletin board and walls. We were visiting her parents for the holidays, and I was always amazed at how her parents kept her room exactly as it was—a living Nicole time capsule. I was fascinated by her room—it was my chance to learn more about the woman I loved—so this wasn't the first time I was snooping around, taking it all in. But this was the first time I saw a tiny slip of paper pinned to the corner of her bulletin board. She had saved the little fortune from a fortune cookie. It said, "The great pleasure in life is doing what people say you cannot do."

You can probably guess how Nicole reacted when I shared my dream of starting a design museum with her. She didn't think I was crazy. She always told me I had to follow my heart. What an amazing example she set for me. Not everyone agreed. There are always going to be folks telling you you can't do it, or it has already been done, or you're making a huge mistake. The key is finding your response to these negative messages and continuing to move forward. These folks are the naysayers.

I experienced four types of naysayers. There were people who said my idea already existed, so I should stop. There were people who claimed what they were doing was better, and so, I should stop. There were people who were very worried about me because this was a huge life risk, and they thought I should stop. And there were people telling me this was impossible, or it was possible, but I wasn't the person who could do it, so— you guessed it—I should just stop.

I knew there were other design museums around the world —I visited many of them. But this was something we heard a lot: *why were we starting another design museum, when there already were design museums?* Folks would mainly point to the Cooper Hewitt National Design Museum in New York City, a beautiful museum that I've visited many times. It's in a Victorian mansion in the city. Every time I visited New York, I would try to visit the Cooper Hewitt. The thing is, I could never convince anyone to come with me. Neither friends nor family wanted to go to a design museum across town in an old mansion.

In Boston, there wasn't a design museum yet, but in 2007, the Institute of Contemporary Art (ICA) hosted one of Cooper Hewitt's touring exhibitions on design. Titled *Design Life Now,* it featured beautiful examples of contemporary design, mainly architecture, product, and graphic design. In the year prior, the ICA made a huge splash in Boston. When I first visited and became a member of the museum in the early 2000s, it was in a tiny space in Boston's Back Bay, next to an old firehouse, with barely enough room to put on a proper exhibition.

In 2006, they moved into a gorgeous new building on Boston's waterfront. The ICA was an inspiration to me—their rags-to-riches story was something out of a startup fairytale. I once heard their Executive Director Jill Medvedow talk about how they only had $5,000 in their bank account when they decided to make the big attempt at raising millions to construct and create a new world-class museum in Boston.

I visited *Design Life Now* at the ICA six times. Twice with Derek. I was so excited to see the work I loved, and the type of work I was doing as a young designer, on display in a museum! There were products on pedestals and architectural models on display. This was a dream come true. As I walked through the high-ceilinged galleries, I had not yet fully conceived the idea for Design Museum Boston, but it's clear to me now that this experience helped plant the seed. *Design Life Now* was the first and last exhibition focused on design the ICA produced at the new building. Their exhibitions were still amazing. I visited a show celebrating the work of a prolific tattoo artist that felt like I was looking at inked skin stretched on the gallery walls—it was incredible. But for some reason, they stopped producing exhibitions on design. I often wonder, *if they had continued, would the Design Museum exist?* Perhaps I would have just been happy visiting the ICA a few times a year to see design on display.

Then there was the crown jewel of the Boston museum scene, the Museum of Fine Arts. My naysayers would often say, *the MFA has a design curator and a design collection—Boston doesn't need you.* It's true that the MFA has a great design collection—nothing like the Cooper Hewitt—but much like the design museum in New York, their collection is very focused on furniture and decorative arts. So when people told me that my idea for a design museum in Boston wouldn't work because the Cooper Hewitt existed in New York, the ICA did one design exhibition (that was rented from the Cooper Hewitt), and because the MFA had some post-modern chairs on display, it made me realize that I had my work cut out for me to better share what we were trying to do with Design Museum Boston. We wanted to make design accessible to everyone and infuse it into people's minds as a creative process that can apply to all things, not just chairs and teapots. We believe all humans are designers, they just don't know it yet.

With all due respect to the three museums mentioned above, traditional museums aren't always known for being the most accessible places to learn. For example, if you live in New York, how many times have you ever been to the Cooper Hewitt? Once a year? Once every two years? Locking design away in an old mansion was not my idea of educating the public on the transformative power of design in our lives. Plus, we wanted to give way more context—design needs context since it's so integrated into every part of our existence. As a designer, I loved the design exhibitions I saw at the Cooper Hewitt, ICA, and MFA, but they were essentially exhibits filled with examples of design sitting on white pedestals and displayed behind glass. We wanted to make design real by showing how it is done, showing who it is done by, and showing the impact design has on people, society, the economy, and the environment. Design is art, and you can display it as art, but we wanted to do more.

All that said, the easiest argument for our idea was location. There was not yet a design museum in Boston, and we wanted to change that. We knew from our experience in the industry and from being leaders in the design community that designers in Greater Boston were designing things that were visited, used, and seen around the world. Boston was a small city, but it was punching above its weight class in terms of creativity and design—design was a net export from Boston. At the time, the city was known for sports, higher learning, life sciences, and history—we wanted to add design to that list. Plus, if New York was going to have a design museum, you could bet Boston was going to have one too.

————

I may have expected people to second guess whether the world needed another design museum and whether we needed one in Boston. But I didn't expect to receive an email from Tom Keane, the Executive Director of the Boston Society of Architects (BSA). Derek's open mic move at the DIGMA meeting turned a lot of heads. People in high places were now aware of what we were trying to do. Tom's email didn't say much. He was interested in our idea and wanted to meet to discuss it. We set a date, December 14, 2009, at 5:30 pm, to meet at his office in The Architect's Building. The Boston Society of Architects is the Boston chapter of the American Institute of Architects, the premier professional organization for architects. It's much like the professional organization for industrial designers, IDSA, of which Derek and I ran the Boston chapter. But that's about where the similarities end. The BSA is one of the most active, well-funded, and impactful AIA chapters. They're not AIA Boston. They're the BSA. And when I checked their publicly available tax documentation before the meeting, I learned their annual budget was in the millions.

On a cold, wet, New England evening, I arrived outside the Architect's Building a bit early to meet Derek and chat before going in to meet with Tom. We often did this—a quick check-in before the meeting to make sure we were on the same page. Since we had no idea what this meeting was about, that was going to be key. But Derek was running late—remember, at this point, we were both still working corporate design jobs outside the city. I didn't worry. I was just glad there were two of us for these kinds of meetings. Then Derek texted me (likely while driving) that there was no way he was going to make it on time and that I should just go in, so we weren't both late.

I got buzzed into the small lobby and took the elevator up to Tom's floor. He met me in the elevator lobby—Tom, a rather tall man and large presence in a full suit and tie, was a stark contrast to me in my jeans, winter jacket, and backpack. He led me into his office. It was small, but only because he was so big and because (like most offices before digital files were truly a thing) it was filled with stacks of paper, books, and file folders. Cramped in that little office, we sat, and Tom said, "So, tell me about what you're working on." I was very used to this, so I went into pitch mode. Me, my business partner, and a handful of board members and volunteers were working to start a new museum in Boston focused on design. That's about as far as I got before Tom chimed in: "Do you know much about the Boston Society of Architects?" I did not.

Tom shared the history of the BSA. It was founded in 1867 before the American Institute of Architects was formed, and later, it merged into the AIA as one of the largest and most active professional architecture communities in the world. As I contemplated what he was saying and the impressiveness of it, he continued, "Now, let me show you what we're working on." With that, he repositioned his chair a bit and moved his monitor so I could see from my little guest chair. He pulled up a PowerPoint presentation, and there it was, right on the first slide: "MODA, The Museum of Design & Architecture," with a rendering of a beautiful brick building. My heart sank into my toes, then down into the first-floor lobby, and out the door into the Boston December cold. The BSA was working to launch a design museum in Boston.

I don't know why, but sometimes it's easier to keep your cool when your heart has completely left your body. I listened intently to Tom's presentation. They were close to signing a lease on a 16,000-square-foot space neatly nestled between the bustling Financial District and Boston's up-and-coming Seaport neighborhood. It was a prime location. They had an equally compelling vision for exhibitions, events, and more. Clearly, there was a focus on displaying architecture (this was the Boston Society of Architects after all), but their stated goal was to cover all areas of design in their programming. I got the message that this was all very close to happening. I can only assume now that this was Tom's professional courtesy meeting —he was more than insinuating that our little ragtag effort to start Design Museum Boston was either doomed to fail or destined to be eclipsed by this multi-million-dollar effort.

I had a lot of thoughts, a few of which were, "Where the hell is Derek?" The others were a scramble of, "Well, we're done. We're toast. Maybe we should try to collaborate with Tom and the BSA. Maybe they'd hire us. But this isn't exactly our vision. How accessible and community-oriented is this effort?" and on and on and on. It's amazing how many thoughts you can have in under two seconds. But the first thing I actually said out loud was pretty petty—what can I say, I was upset. I said, "This is so cool, but you know, MODA already exists. There's the Museum of Design Atlanta." Tom was nonplussed and shared that the name didn't matter at this point—the point was this was happening. Boston was going to have a design museum. Construction had already begun on the building.

Just then, Derek arrived—thankfully, because who knows where I would have taken the conversation at that point. As he entered the office, I turned so Tom couldn't see my face and gave him the 911 emergency eyes. He gave me the, "What the hell is going on?" look back as he shook Tom's hand and had nowhere to sit. Tom gave a standing Derek a brief run-through of what I had just seen—so I got to see my dream die all over again. But with Derek there, it was easier to feign excitement rather than wallow in all my worry. Derek was always so good at interacting with people, regardless of what they were talking about. He asked questions, had Tom dig deeper into points, and opened up space for me to get over my feelings and be genuinely interested in the idea—it was a great vision. I started thinking, "Is it important that we (as in Derek and I) start a design museum in Boston, or that a design museum comes into existence, period?"

Derek so charmed Tom and changed the tenor of the whole meeting that I somehow found myself agreeing to grab drinks with Tom to talk further. The three of us donned our coats and made our way outside—I thought, "Oh good, I can grab my frozen heart off the icy street and put it back in my chest. I wonder if it still works?" At a nearby bar, the conversation turned to answer the question, *how do we collaborate and make something amazing for Boston?* With Derek's charm and the addition of alcohol, I was getting over the intense ownership I had of the idea, and I was ready to make something cool together. Tom was smiling and laughing and agreeing with pretty much everything we said. We could bring another facet to their effort. We had an active online community of a few thousand people who were eager to help make a museum that was accessible to the public and covered every aspect of design, from architecture to graphic design, and more. We finished the night agreeing that we should continue talking and figure out a way to collaborate. I left thinking, "Is this how the world works? Maybe I have a new job coming my way, I don't have to start this, but I can help bring it into existence, backed by a huge organization with a big fancy budget."

We shook hands with Tom and parted ways. As Derek and I silently walked down the street, and even though I was filled with more doubt than ever, I turned to Derek and quietly said, "We're still doing our thing, right?" He immediately and confidently replied, "Oh, definitely." Still, the next day, I emailed Tom and cc'd Derek, saying thanks for having us over and sharing the vision for MODA. We were excited about the idea, and we were ready to continue the conversation and see how we could get involved. Days and weeks passed with no reply—I followed up a few times—but we never once heard from Tom Keane again. It was official. We had competition, and competitors are always going to be naysayers.

———

The most difficult naysayers for me were somewhat paradoxical. The people who supported me most were most concerned for my future. Everything in life has an opportunity cost—meaning if you're doing something, that means you aren't doing something else. And as much as creative entrepreneurs might be able to stretch, working a full-time job and building a business on the side, we have limited time and capacity. In my case, it meant, if I kept pursuing the Design Museum idea, eventually I'd have to leave my extremely stable corporate job—along with the paycheck and health insurance

—at Bose Corporation. And that was risky because who knew what was in store for the Design Museum? I certainly didn't.

Jaime Read, the professor who Derek and I first shared the Design Museum idea with, was very supportive of our vision, but his first reaction was, "Why would you two young designers, who have great jobs and amazing careers ahead of you, want to throw that all away on an unknown?" He then proceeded to throw all his support behind what we were working on, but that was his first response. People can be your biggest supporters and your toughest naysayers at the same time—it can be very confusing. My parents were my biggest supporters. My mom taught me how to use my creativity, and I grew up with my Dad telling me I could do anything I set my mind to. But they were worried.

My mom would question how I was planning to make money and have health insurance so that I could build a life and have a family. She often asked, "How do you even know how to do all of this?" What I heard was, "What happens if you make a mistake you can't recover from?" My dad was equally worried. He called me one night while I was making the hour-long car commute from Bose to my apartment and flat-out asked me, "Why do you want to do this? You have a job, a paycheck, a pension, a 401k, a career, and everything you need to set yourself up for life. Why throw that all away for something like an idea for a museum?" He was telling me to stop and focus on the sure thing—he was worried about me, simple as that.

My parents are children of Great-Depression-era parents. They grew up with very little. My grandparents had very little education or opportunity. My father's and my namesake, my Grandpa Sam, fought in France on D-Day, came home from the war wounded, and worked in a factory for the rest of his life. My father was the only child among his siblings, my mother, and her siblings to go to college. My parent's goal was to lift themselves out of poverty, create stability and predictability, and then build a life where they could provide way more opportunity for their children (me and my siblings) than they ever had. It wasn't exactly a mission where you wanted to invite any kind of risk. My parents were essentially laser-focused on building educational opportunities and generational wealth for me, my brother, and my sister.

I'm truly in awe of where they came from and what they've done and accomplished in two-thirds of a lifetime. I never wanted for anything as a kid. I wouldn't say I was a spoiled rich kid, but it's all relative, and you might. My parents calculated how to best set their kids up for success in this world. Education was paramount, I went to great public schools for K-12. I could have any book I wanted, ever. If I would read it, they would buy it for me, no matter what. I went to great public schools and an amazing college. My parents set me up in every way to succeed in life in America—I just needed to follow the plan, and I'd be set for life. Leaving a high-paying job and changing careers to start a nonprofit museum was not part of the plan. I can see from my parents' perspective that they weren't just worried. To them, they were watching their son throw away all their preparation, just as they had gotten him to the promised land.

I had different plans, of course. I wanted to take all the love, money, and privilege they bestowed on me and do something meaningful in this world—not just sit at a desk in the corporate world for thirty years. And I know I can only write that sentence because of what they've done for me. President John Adams once said, "I must study war and politics so that my children shall be free to study commerce, agriculture and other practicalities, so that their children can study painting, poetry and other fine things." I can confidently say the Design Museum only exists because of my parents' support and because, in the early days, they questioned whether the idea was something I should put my energy behind. Was it worth the opportunity cost? My answer was always, "Yes."

In a particularly fun exchange, my Dad, brother, and I were talking about careers. My Dad liked to remind me that I could work anywhere I wanted. "You could be a real asset for someone. You could work for Apple. You could work for Steve Jobs!"

"I am Steve Jobs!" I yelled back, with way too much confidence. I tried to explain that I had a vision for something new and, like Steve Jobs, I was working so hard to make it succeed. I didn't really think I was equivalent to Steve Jobs, but my confident outburst ended the conversation on whether I should continue on my entrepreneurial journey.

———

Then there were the folks who told us that what we were trying to do was impossible. Either it wasn't possible, or maybe it was possible, but two young designers with no money and no experience weren't the ones to do it. I mean, what would you say to a pair of twenty-somethings who told you they were going to start a museum during the worst economy since the Great Depression? People said we were crazy, that we were naive and unrealistic, or worse: they patronized us with a verbal pat on the head. "Great idea," they'd say, as they pushed us out the door.

Right around this time, there was a blue-ribbon effort to create another museum, a museum of Boston's past, present, and future. Named *The Boston Museum,* the team behind it included everyone you'd want in your corner: government officials, CEOs, real estate developers, million-dollar donors, and more. They even had a choice site locked in adjacent to the newly opened Rose Kennedy Greenway, the beautiful public park that replaced an elevated highway and snakes through and around Downtown Boston. Safdie Architects, a world-renowned architecture firm even designed the building for it. But The Boston Museum faltered in the tough economic climate. Even with the smartest, wealthiest Bostonians behind it, it failed. If they couldn't do it, how could we?

There's a bonus fifth type of naysayer. There are the people who say your business idea already exists, your competitors, the people who care so deeply about you that they don't want you to make a mistake, folks who call you crazy because this is impossible, and finally, number five: you. The day after our *Prepare to Launch* event, I was sharing a meal with my Mom and brother Steve. They were still in town visiting after helping us pull off the epic event. I was tired and still in disbelief and filled with all sorts of self-doubt. I said, "That was great, but we have nothing, no money, no building, nothing."

It takes real effort to convince yourself, to overcome self-doubt, and move forward. I'm sorry to say that work is never done. There will always be lingering doubt, and you'll be your own naysayer, so the work doesn't end—but through your co-founding team, your community, and your early wins, I promise it will get easier. After hearing my despair, my mom simply said, "You have a dream and people who believe in you, keep going."

It's hard to field the naysayers, especially when you're one of them, and you hear your own doubts echoing in their words. It's the other side of the coin from all the people who support you. It could be that your chasing your dream is threatening in some way, or they're worried sick about you, or they're so married to the status quo, they can't see the world for what it could be. Ray Goforth, the Executive Director of the Society of Professional Engineering Employees in Aerospace, once said, "There are two types of people who will tell you that you cannot make a difference in this world: those who are afraid to try and those who are afraid you will succeed."

So how can you prepare yourself and your business to handle the naysayers? I recommend reflecting on chapters one, two, and three of this book. You've done the work to convince yourself, now you need to be your own biggest supporter. You've recruited unconditional support from co-founders who have your back no matter what. You've built a community around this idea, and they care deeply about this effort. If you do this right, the people who support you will dramatically outweigh the naysayers.

Deep down, I actually liked the competitive naysayers because it gave me a reason to think critically about what made Design Museum Boston special and how I could evolve the idea to outsmart them. What businesses and organizations are out there doing what you want to be doing or something close to what you're doing? Emulate them, and then innovate on what they're doing—figure out what makes you different. And by the way, it's okay if the thing that makes you different is the fact that your business has you (or you and your team)! No one else has you.

Don't wait for others to be the first ones to confront you as naysayers. Anticipate this, and question yourselves. Write down how you would respond to each of the five types of naysayers. Developing your responses as a team will hone your idea and tame the mounting doubt that naysayers are so good at stirring up. Let's look at our example creative entrepreneurial adventures and see how we can respond to the naysayers. There's our cupcake show and online ordering business, *For Cupcake's Sake.* We keep hearing our naysayers say, "There are tons of bakeries in town and so many businesses online making and selling cupcakes to order." We respond, "Yes, but we've built a strong local following. We've made connections with local high-end hotels and corporations to supply cupcakes for special events. These folks aren't just ordering from some invisible online bakery—they're building relationships with our team and our brand." Or, "Sure, there are a lot of online mail-order cupcake shops, but over the years, we've been baking with organic ingredients, and while cupcakes may never truly be healthy, we have a story to tell around healthier cupcakes that we think is intriguing enough to drive orders. In fact, we already have six orders from wellness companies, and when we surveyed those buyers, they said they found us because they care about organic ingredients." Practically every idea already exists. That's just the reality of the world we live in. Don't let that fact stop you from developing something special.

Look at *Art Scouts.* We're developing this youth-focused arts nonprofit on the side (we all currently have full-time jobs). We've done a handful of workshops at the local community center and in collaboration with the children's museum in town. Someone close to one of our founders says, "Why are you spending your precious time on this? You have a job that pays well in the field you studied in college—you've already made it!" It's always difficult, especially with those closest to us to explain why we're working so hard on *Art Scouts*. But because we've reflected on and anticipated naysayers to our creative entrepreneurship, we're ready. One of our founders says, "I love my job and what I do. That's partially why I want to make sure young people have the chance I had to learn and love art. Plus, life is too short to not do what you love. There's a great quote from civil rights leader Howard Thurman, 'Don't ask what the world needs. Ask what makes you come alive, and go do it. Because what the world needs is people who have come alive.'" Maybe they'll buy that, and maybe they won't, but at least we're confident doing what we know in our hearts is the right thing to do. Full disclosure, that quote from Howard Thurman is one of my wife Nicole's favorites and is always posted on our refrigerator.

Who wouldn't want Nicole to pursue her dream of being a ceramic artist? The quick answer? It doesn't matter. She gets to decide. It's you and your team who get to decide this for yourselves. The naysayers are only right if you agree with them. Figure out your responses—why you're doing this, what makes you special—then write them down, and deal with the naysayers with poise and grace. That way you'll be ready to learn from them rather than be hindered by their words.

CHAPTER 5

Absolutely Love Change

It's the only constant in this adventure we call life.

"A pivot is a change in strategy without a change in vision."
— Eric Ries, author, entrepreneur

In early 2010, I was feeling a bit like this was going to be impossible. I mean, the executive director of the largest design organization in the city had just told me that they were creating a design museum in Boston. How were two 27-year-olds going to do this? We did what we did best: asked for help and leaned on our community. Most importantly, we weren't afraid of change—we made a pivot that changed everything.

Kim Poliquin is a project architect in Boston designing residential, commercial, and institutional projects around the world. She started her career in 2000 in New York but eventually found her way to Cambridge Seven Associates in

Cambridge, MA, where she designed epic projects like the House of Blues in Boston and the Hard Rock Cafe in Waikiki Beach, Hawaii. Then everything changed. The housing bubble burst in the United States, and by 2008, a subprime mortgage crisis was in full effect. The country, and the world, was plunged into the Great Recession, the most severe economic meltdown since the Great Depression. Everything ground to a halt—consumer spending dropped like a stone as more and more people were laid off from their jobs. Unemployment hit levels and durations not seen since the 1930s. With all the economic insecurity, building projects were paused, delayed, or canceled. Thus, Kim found herself somewhere she never expected: laid off and out of a job.

Nineteenth-century UK prime minister Benjamin Disraeli said, "Change is inevitable. Change is constant." I wholeheartedly agree—the sooner you learn to embrace and love change, the sooner you'll align yourself and your actions with the natural way of the world. In 2009, Kim experienced a big change, losing her job, but rather than sit idle and lament her disrupted career, she took action and made a change of her own.

In June 2009, she founded SHIFTboston, an organization (a platform, really) for creating and sharing ideas that improve the human urban experience. She pivoted her career from designing the built environment to creating an environment for ideas that could change the city and the world. She didn't see the recession as a moment to survive; she saw it as a critical moment to stop, think, re-envision the urban realm, and in doing so, help move Boston forward.

The primary organizing mechanism Kim envisioned was a series of open idea competitions that would challenge folks to think differently about Boston. Kim wanted to ask, "What if big change could happen in Boston?" to the most creative people in the city, and enable those ideas to drive real transformation. The inaugural challenge was the *SHIFTboston Ideas Competition*—with the open call, SHIFTboston sought, "wild provocative visions that would enhance and electrify the urban experience in Boston." There was no area off limits, no idea too wild. That first competition garnered 141 submissions from fourteen states and sixteen countries. Kim and her team of volunteers recruited an all-star jury of designers, public officials, and urban planners to review the submission, choose finalists, and pick a winner—the winning project would receive $1,000 and be part of a marketing campaign around the city.

On January 14, 2010, Derek and I were there at the Institute for Contemporary Art as the finalists were announced and presented. The ideas were amazing. There was a proposal to create floating, mobile parks to activate the waterfront, a network of food-producing gardens around the city, an idea to draw a blue line on buildings and city infrastructure that would denote where the sea level would rise to, and more. The winner was called *TUTS* or *Tremont Underground Theater Space*. Designers Sapir Ng and Andrzej Zarzycki asked, "What if the abandoned Tremont Street Subway Tunnel became an interactive social environment?" They imagined turning the old tunnel—part of North America's oldest subway system— into art galleries, restaurants, meeting spaces, and a theater. It was genius and exactly the kind of inspiring idea that Kim was looking for. It could change the fabric of the city.

The SHIFTboston forum was magical. Derek and I were inspired to see so many designers, innovators, and leaders in one auditorium, talking about how design could change people's lives in Boston. Kim took a major life change and turned it into an inspiring moment of positive change for everyone around her. As she said at the forum, "We believe a collective desire to push boundaries and challenge the familiar are the necessary seeds with which to grow a more dynamic city!" She sensed that change was possible in that moment, and she made it happen.

———

Change can be scary, or it can be beautiful, or both, and everything in between. But either way, change is inevitable. Harness it. Learn to love change because what you're doing now isn't what you're going to be doing forever—that's just not how the world works. Change breeds ideas, opportunities, and innovation. Change is good and essential for you to thrive. Your idea is just an idea until it meets the market, and you adapt it to survive and succeed.

Derek and I were at the SHIFTboston forum in January 2010—not just because it was a great place to be. We submitted our own entry to the competition. The competition was announced a month after we officially incorporated our nonprofit. At that point, only a few people knew what Derek and I were trying to do. But we had kind of a clever idea. We learned that the effort behind The Boston Museum on the Rose Kennedy Greenway was waning, so we thought, "What if the Design Museum Boston rose from its ashes? What if there was a design museum on the Greenway?" We started dreaming about and sketching our ideal design museum building. It would be open and inviting, welcoming to everyone, and a place you'd want to visit multiple times a year because of the cafe, restaurant, social meeting areas, and, of course, the world-class exhibitions and events. Once again we reached out to our community on designingamuseum.org. We asked people what they wanted in a design museum. What should it look like? What were examples of museum buildings they loved?

As word spread in the online community that we were designing a concept for our future building, one of our members and close friends, Bruce Lee, reached out and asked if we needed help visualizing the concept. Bruce is a super-talented industrial designer and 3D concept designer. He could make anything using 3D CAD software and render it to create photorealistic images you'd swear on your life were real. We started meeting regularly with Bruce in person and on Skype, sharing our vision, sketches, and community's ideas. Bruce got to work creating the overall building and landscape around it, with just enough detail to be convincing. He added real buildings around the Boston Museum site with people walking around, enjoying the galleries, and sitting at the cafe.

For Derek and me, it was like watching our dream become a reality in real-time. The act of visualizing your outcome can be so powerful. It can sustain and drive you toward your goals. And once Bruce finished, we had our dream manifested, rendered in photorealistic detail, sitting in a real place in the city. It was all glass but with enough design details reminiscent of a traditional museum. It was like a traditional marble-columned museum had a baby with an Apple Store. From the street, you could see directly into the galleries, making that beautiful design accessible—you'd be drawn in to learn more and enjoy. Bruce did an incredible job. We pulled some content from our vision statement, designed our digital presentation boards, and submitted everything to SHIFTboston right before the December 2009 deadline. Now we had our vision book and a concept design for a building on a real site in Boston. We knew we wouldn't be able to create such an epic construction project, but we were dreaming and getting our community to dream right along with us—and a dream can be a powerful thing.

Acquiring or leasing a building was in our vision statement from the beginning. A museum needs a space, right? One of the pages in our vision book had a simple photo of a brick wall, a visual metaphor for us and anyone reading the statement that we were aiming toward something every museum needs: a brick-and-mortar space to connect with their audience. Our goal was to make the right connections, raise some money, and get a space—something much more modest than Bruce's beautiful design. We really just needed to lease some kind of simple space to get started. The connections were plentiful. Derek and I would use our vacation days to take time off work and load up a day off with as many meetings for the museum as we could. Getting meetings wasn't the issue; money was the issue. We were in a recession, so money was scarce. Now that I've run the Design Museum through two recessions over thirteen years, I can tell you the lack of discretionary spending on philanthropy is a void so real you almost feel like you can touch it. The folks who really could give were still giving in those days, but certainly not to totally new ideas with an untested team. People loved our idea, but the economy was in a bad place.

We had a lot swirling around in our minds. The Boston Museum was folding. The richest, most connected people in Boston couldn't figure this out. The meeting with Tom Keane and the BSA's plan to open a brick-and-mortar design museum (their building was literally made of bricks and mortar) weighed heavily on us. Should we quit? I thought about that a lot, I assume Derek did as well. But the funny thing is, we never talked about stopping. We were way too passionate about the vision of making design more accessible to the public to forget about it—together, Derek, I, and our little founding team were like a star ready to go supernova. Plus, we had this incredible group of volunteers and board members who believed in the vision and mission of Design Museum Boston, as well as a community of thousands backing us up and encouraging us to push on.

The BSA was creating a traditional museum, and from what we saw, it was shaping up to be a museum of architecture for architects. Competition has a way of focusing my thoughts. It actually has a way of narrowing the realm of possibilities because the playing field seems to shrink a bit. All of a sudden, the range of what's possible goes from infinite to something less than infinite, and that helps focus me toward paths that can work in the marketplace. If the BSA was going to do a building, maybe we should do something different, something more nimble that people could connect with more easily. One of the problems with traditional museums is they're actually not that accessible. You must actually go to them to experience their programming and content. The tech community was building a future where things came to us: Uber rides, grocery delivery, and streaming movies at home. Increasingly, the world was in our pockets with the iPhone and all these connected services, and therefore, the world was wherever each of us was at any given time.

Derek and I were meeting two to four times a week—either one-on-one or with our volunteer team. We were talking on the phone daily and emailing and texting throughout the day. We started thinking and talking about what was holding us back and what was going to hold us back. How could we compete with the BSA at a time when starting a new museum seemed utterly impossible? I was laser-focused on the business elements. I started an MBA program at Babson College the same month Derek and I hit submit on our business incorporation.

I often used the Design Museum as a case study for my class projects. I started thinking, "What are the biggest costs going to be for our little museum?" Likely the same big expense for any museum, the physical building. For a building in Boston or a space in a building in Boston, we would likely have a hefty lease. I assumed we would need a build-out to be able to mount exhibitions and hold events. Then we'd need a lot of marketing dollars to get people to learn about us and entice them to come to our space. We could have the coolest space in the world with the best exhibitions, but if no one knew about us, what was the point? So what if we had neither a space nor a marketing budget? Because we had neither.

In Derek's travels, he experienced an old concept made new: pop-up retail stores. Pop-up shops date back hundreds of years—think seasonal markets in the village square. They hit modern trend status as an alternative to brick-and-mortar stores during the economic downturn of the late 2000s. A retailer or maker without a shop would temporarily set up in an unused space for a short amount of time. Often, they were aligned with events or specific holidays, like a greeting card designer popping up a shop right before Mother's Day. The maker didn't own the space; they were just borrowing it so they could connect with customers at a particular place and time. The insight hit us like a ton of bricks.

We could be a pop-up museum. There might not be money for us to lease a space, but as we walked around downtown Boston during the Great Recession, there was space everywhere. There were empty retail spaces sitting idle, underutilized public spaces, building lobbies, parks—the whole city could be the museum, and the museum could be everywhere! Do you know what else is everywhere? Design. It's our clothes, shoes, phones, coffeemakers, magazines, websites, homes, buildings, streets, communities, cities, institutions, services—it's everything, everywhere. We got to thinking, *maybe the design museum should be everywhere as well.*

We had something here, something big—and we had the holidays at the end of 2009 to let the idea build in our minds. As we often did, we sought out a conversation with a trusted advisor to test and hone the idea with their feedback. We reached out to the Creative Economy Director, Jason Shupbach, to discuss this new direction. He was so helpful throughout our startup process, and he knew the lay of the land. He was there at the DIGMA meeting when Derek grabbed the microphone. He was aware of the BSA's effort to launch MODA. He was even a member on designingamuseum.org.

We met at an old-school Boston bar right across from Boston City Hall on January 5, 2010. Derek and I arrived that evening equal parts dejected by the situation with the BSA and buzzing because of our new idea. Jason knew we met with Tom Keane shortly before the holidays and asked how we were holding up. Over beers, I shared that we were quite shocked that there was a multi-million dollar effort to establish a design museum in Boston. Despite the surprise, we still wanted to continue because our mission was more about accessibility, and now, we thought we had an approach that could match that mission.

There was a pause as Jason waited for us to describe the new approach. I broke the silence: "We don't need a building." He met our previous silence with his own as he briefly thought it over, then replied, "You're right!" We shared the idea of becoming the first nomadic museum—Derek summed it up nicely: "We can turn the museum inside out and turn the entire city into a design museum." Jason loved it. He shared ideas for where we could pop up and how this could reach audiences everywhere. This approach could bring design inspiration and education to high schools, public buildings, corporate lobbies, and even outside in parks. This was also a way to start up quicker and gain a first-mover advantage, cementing our concept in the minds of Bostonians as the first design museum in the city. Plus, with this nomadic approach, we could run circles around traditional museum efforts since we could move around the city, connecting with new audiences in places they already go, while others were tied to a single location—a ball and chain with a very short chain.

On our way to that very bar, we walked through Downtown Crossing—Boston's downtown retail core—and we saw tons of empty retail spaces. Companies were folding during the recession, and the spaces were just sitting there, sad and empty. Some empty shops did have some life/ There was a program called *Boston Art Windows* where art was displayed in the windows of unused retail spaces.

Jason loved the pivot to a building-less, nomadic museum, and as always, he was willing to help. He knew who ran the *Boston Art Windows* program. He pointed across the street at City Hall and said, "I'm going to connect you with Randi Lathrop over at the BRA—she spearheads the Boston Art Windows program and can help you secure a temporary space in Downtown Crossing. I'm sure of it." The BRA, or Boston Redevelopment Authority, was the powerful central planning office within the city and, therefore, was connected to every building owner, retail operation, real estate development firm, and architecture firm in Boston.

We were thrilled by the possibility of a meeting and testing out our nomadic approach in an unused retail space in Downtown Crossing. This is how we moved the idea forward, one meeting at a time, sharing our thoughts and ideas and being open to others' feedback and ideas—and getting that next connection to someone else who could help. With Jason's enthusiasm, we went a step further and shared the idea with our board of directors and then with members of our online community.

Even before this idea to pivot to a nomadic approach, we were exploring different taglines and slogans, and we were loving "Design is everywhere." With our new approach, we added, "So are we," as a nod to our new nomadic nature and to honor our growing community. People loved the idea. It just made sense. It clicked for everyone. Design is everywhere, so why lock it away in a building? Design is everywhere, so the design museum should be, too. One of our board members, Robert Reimann, commented that it was the right idea for the right time. Amazon was a retailer without any physical retail stores. Uber was a car service that owned no vehicle fleet. Design museum would be a museum that owned no physical space—and that would be our strength in the market.

Buzz was building. Our pivot turned our effort into a story about innovation during an economic crisis. Plus, there was a bonus: a David vs. Goliath competition between our idea and the BSA's effort to launch a brick-and-mortar museum. That's really why we heard from Christopher Muther at the Boston Globe. The pivot, the duality of Design Museum Boston and the BSA, and our planned launch party in March together made us newsworthy. I kicked off the interview with Christopher, putting our pivot front and center: "We thought we needed to get a building to house our museum. We realized pretty quickly that we wouldn't be able to get a building because it would take years to raise the kind of money we would need, and this isn't exactly a great time to be hitting people up for money." Muther added, "It is a good time, however, to be in the market for empty storefronts. The two 27-year-old designers scuttled their dreams of a brick-and-mortar museum and took another path: Create a nomadic museum that exists in empty storefronts around the state and bring design to retail areas."

The article also quotes Beate Becker, Founding Director of DIGMA, the Design Industry Group of Massachusetts: "We had wanted to do it ourselves, but this is ideal because Sam and Derek have a tremendous amount of energy for this project, and they've made it a reality in an incredibly short amount of time." ShiftBoston is even mentioned in the article, along with our Goliath, the BSA. Chris wrote, "Coincidentally there are plans in the works for a second design museum in Boston. The Boston Society of Architects announced it is planning its own museum, part of its new location at Russia Wharf in Fort Point Channel. The BSA entered into a non-binding agreement for the first two floors of a building, which would also include offices and meeting spaces for the organization. If its plan comes to fruition, it would occupy the space in 2011."

The Globe article solidified our pivot, thrust us into the spotlight, and celebrated our first-mover advantage as the first effort to start a design museum in Boston. We were doing something no one had done before, and we celebrated the launch of our nomadic museum at West End Johnnie's to raucous applause. Pivoting to this new model changed how we thought about everything. It was like deconstructing something into its component parts and only keeping the most necessary pieces. We could let go of the rest and be free to innovate. It was like smashing a pane of glass and then reassembling it into a beautiful stained glass window of possibilities—when you looked through the glass now, everything looked different and interesting.

—————

Embrace change. It's easy to say, harder to do. It's okay to love your idea, just don't fall in love with it. Put your idea out there in some form—a prototype or a test—and see what your community falls in love with. That's what matters. In our case, people wanted to celebrate good design and increase the public's design awareness; they didn't specifically want a museum building. They fell in love with the vision, not the approach. When we pivoted, they fell in love with the whole thing. If you get married to your original idea and resist any changes, the business environment could easily shut you down. The design process is very useful here. You should constantly be gathering information that feeds inspiration into your idea generation.

From there, design a prototype or test to put your idea out there in a real way. Then see what happens. Do people love it? Will they pay for it? Are they telling their friends about it? No? Rinse and repeat. Stay nimble, especially in the early days. Stay loose in the beginning, and only solidify the parts of your business that are absolutely necessary. How can you start up with the least amount of physical assets like property or equipment? Do you really need your own physical space for your business? Establishing and selling online is so much less asset-intensive and keeps you flexible—it's a quicker and less risky way to start up. If what you're doing does require specialized, expensive equipment, is there a co-working space you can join where that equipment is shared? Or is there a similar but different-enough business that has excess capacity on their equipment that would be willing to let you lease that capacity? I recommend limiting your investment in physical assets for as long as possible until you find your product-market fit and gain traction with customers.

You're going to learn a lot from your first test—putting yourself out there is going to be super scary. You know this because it was already scary to even talk about your idea with another human being. If you go into a test with an open mindset, you're setting yourself up to learn. You don't need to own every part of your idea. Be open to change, and it'll come to you, I promise. And remember, there's a lot to learn from competitors. They're already doing it. Their efforts are test data mainlined in your design process. The BSA's *Museum of Design and Architecture* gave Derek and me something to innovate around. The competition drove us to think differently.

Your pivot might look like ours. It might mean tweaking one element of your original idea to connect with a customer base that loves what you're offering. We had a vision to inspire and educate the public about design's impact on our lives, we pivoted from a strategy built around a physical space to becoming a nomadic museum, and it catalyzed our growth in ways I could never have imagined. Your pivot might look like Instagram's or Slack's—each took an element of their original idea and made it their whole business. Instagram came out of founder Kevin Systrom and team's location-based check-in app, Burbn. On the app, you could check in at places, post your plans for the evening, and share photos. Burbn didn't catch on, but people absolutely loved sharing photos. They pivoted to what we now know as Instagram today.

Slack was a similar story. It started as a game developer, working on a title called Glitch, a so-called never-ending game. The game didn't prove viable, but during development, they created a custom online chatting tool to keep their team organized across different countries. Everyone loved using it! They pivoted the operation away from games to asynchronous communication, and they launched Slack. Your pivot might be an even bigger wholesale change that simply keeps your team intact as you create something totally new. Twitter started as Odeo, a platform for finding and listening to podcasts. Then Apple jumped into the mix and completely changed the podcast listening market. Instead of folding, the Odeo team went into information-gathering and ideation mode. They came up with the idea of microblogging, where folks could share updates and ideas with friends and contacts all over the world in real time. Twitter was born.

Pivoting is as natural for startups as breathing is for humans. Even the BSA had to pivot. After we launched and garnered support as the first design museum in Boston, the BSA's Museum of Design & Architecture never happened. Instead, they opened a new headquarters with event and gallery space opened to the public called BSA Space. We hosted and attended many events at the BSA Space over the years. They featured some amazing exhibitions, including our traveling exhibition on the design and importance of play. Because of our fateful meeting, both visions were changed—ours to become a nomadic museum, theirs to become a public gallery space—and in the end, we became close collaborators in the Boston design community.

At Design Museum Everywhere, the pivot culture of questioning and experimentation—and not being afraid of change—persists today and makes us nearly invincible to changes in the market or competition because we're always adapting, embracing change, and pivoting quickly. The Great Recession of 2008-2010 could have easily been a time when we all gave up. In the wake of another much more trying time —post-World War II—as he was working with other world leaders to form the United Nations, Winston Churchill famously said, "Never let a good crisis go to waste."

Many believe recessions are actually the best time to start something. Yes, there's economic anxiety, but there's also an energy that comes from trying moments like this when the status quo shifts and windows of opportunity seem just a bit more open than usual. Kim Poliquin saw this when she launched SHIFTboston. She knew Boston wasn't going to take the Great Recession lying down, and she made it her mission to share the best, most innovative ideas for how the city could change and improve for the benefit of everyone. Her effort helped create the conditions for change and innovation where an idea like Design Museum Boston could take root and grow.

CHAPTER 6

Distribute Your Ignorance

Spread it around to great effect.

"We now accept the fact that learning is a lifelong process of keeping abreast of change. And the most pressing task is to teach people how to learn."
— Peter Drucker, author, management consultant

We started. We had a vision, shared it with trusted advisors, and built a community. We shared more, got knocked down, pivoted, and rose from the ashes of our original idea with something innovative and exciting that drove our launch and early growth. But as the Globe article pointed out right in the headline, we were two 27-year-old designers with a team that was equally young and inexperienced. We had to figure out what to do next and how to do it, and that was going to take some serious learning.

I was twenty years old when I started working at Bose Corporation, first as an intern, then as a full-time industrial designer. I finished four years of college and trained to be a designer, but as amazing as the experience was at RIT, upon starting my career, I quickly realized that I only knew about 5% of what I really needed to know to be a successful professional designer. I could create and give form to objects, I knew the software programs, and I could certainly communicate my ideas and accept feedback and critique, but I knew very little about business, marketing, manufacturing, materials, processes, etc. I was working for an audio company, and I didn't know what a transducer was, why air was so important to acoustics, what electromagnetic shielding was, how parts are injection molded and then assembled in a factory, or how our products were marketed and sold. My job was to design products based on highly advanced audio technology that could be manufactured in Bose factories, and sold in our stores—my work was connected to almost every aspect of the company, but I knew almost nothing. At least, it felt that way.

I remember during my first few months, I felt frozen with fear. How was I going to do this? But it quickly dawned on me, I knew how to learn. I could read, I could ask questions, and I could explore. I was surrounded by hundreds of experts in so many different fields—I could learn from all of them if I just built relationships and asked good questions. I came up with a plan. I read books and articles online about manufacturing, materials, processes, acoustics, integrated circuits, and engineering. It wasn't enough to become an expert, but I learned just enough so that when I asked that first expert a question, it didn't sound like I knew nothing. I learned enough to ask at least one informed question.

I didn't want any one person at Bose to know just how little I knew, so I distributed my ignorance around the company. I'd introduce myself to an acoustics engineer and sort of pretend I knew what I was talking about (enough to get them talking). I'd ask a couple of questions to get clarity, and then I was on to someone else. I did this for everything, connecting with people in every field and expertise around the corporate campus. Not only was I learning a ton, but I was building a network within the company. You would be amazed how generous people can be with their knowledge—and how they'll tend to like you—when you treat them like an expert and genuinely ask meaningful questions. I was building relationships and learning, and both accelerated me toward success in that job.

———

You may know everything you need to know to launch and grow your startup. If so, I'm happy for you. Congratulations. If you're like me, though, you know nothing (or you know a little). But no one else needs to know that all at once. In fact, I wouldn't even admit that to myself at the time. With Design Museum Boston, we were starting a new nonprofit museum with no nonprofit or museum experience at all. Derek and I were reminded pretty regularly that we were young, naive, and inexperienced.

In our Boston Globe feature, our inexperience was part of the story. For the author, it was an underdog story,—two young, bright-eyed idealists making it happen against the odds. Others weren't so kind. In meetings, folks would openly question how we thought we could pull this off. In one meeting in particular, a consultant on the BSA's MODA project implied that what we were trying to do was impossible and even a little silly given the fact that we were two young designers, and they had a whole team of "adults."

At the time, we thought these naysayers were mean and out of line. But they weren't wrong. We knew absolutely nothing about starting a nonprofit museum. But, like so often is the case, our naïveté was our strength. If we knew everything about what it was going to take, everything we would need to do and sacrifice to bring Design Museum Boston to the world, we probably would have quit from the sheer overwhelming reality we faced. Ignorance is bliss, I guess, or at least, ignorance allows for forward momentum in the face of adversity. I wasn't going to take any of this lying down, and I wasn't going to let our lack of knowledge and experience be the thing that stopped us from achieving our goal of starting a new museum. My college experience may have only taught me a fraction of what I needed to know as an industrial designer, but I learned how to learn, and that is the most important skill for a creative entrepreneur. If you know how to learn, and you practice it regularly, you'll be unstoppable. Here's how I did it—and how I keep doing it because the learning process never stops.

The knowledge is out there. All you need to do is read it. In the years leading up to sharing this idea of starting a museum with Derek, I read everything I could get my hands on about museums, nonprofits, entrepreneurship, and more. We used LegalZoom to register our business on August 20, 2009. A few weeks later, the online service sent us a 300-page book titled *Starting & Building a Nonprofit: A Practical Guide* by Peri H. Pakroo, J.D. It covered everything from taxes to recruiting board members, applying for 501c3 status to employment law, and more. I read it multiple times. It wasn't just a book; it was a guide. As I read it, I applied the knowledge to Design Museum Boston.

I also read books like *The Participatory Museum* by Nina Simon that inspired our programmatic and audience outreach approaches. The museum field was ripe for innovation, and folks like Simon were at the forefront of pushing what museums could be as resources and community gathering points. There's so much to be learned in books. Then there's the Internet! I read article after article about how to start a nonprofit, fundraising, philanthropy, and nonprofit compliance law. There are even specific articles about how to actually start a museum. Google is amazing when you put it in the hands of the curious. And I was a sponge. If I had a thought or question, I'd immediately do a Google search, read a couple of articles, save more for later, and absorb, absorb, absorb.

Then I went to the experts to distribute my ignorance around the nonprofit and museum community in Boston. Much like at Bose, I didn't want anyone in the local industry to know that I truly didn't know much about nonprofit management or fundraising, so I cast a wide net. For example, I wanted to learn a lot more about fundraising—or as I learned from my conversations, what the nonprofit industry calls *development*. I started compiling a list of people from local museums and academic institutions who worked in development with whom I could try to get a call or a meeting.

Sometimes I could get a connection through someone I knew, but most of the time, it was a cold email. I introduced myself and introduced Design Museum Boston with a link to our website and a link to the Globe article for credibility. Then I shared that I was looking to connect with experts to ask some lingering questions about development and how they fund their organizations. They were one such expert I found, and I'd love to buy them lunch or hop on the phone to ask some quick questions. It worked. I secured phone calls and meetings with development professionals in various organizations around Greater Boston, including the fundraising leaders at Massachusetts College of Art and Design, the MIT Museum, and Babson College. I learned a ton from these conversations, including a whole new list of books and online resources to check out. This kind of learning and outreach builds on itself, especially when you simply ask, "What are some of your favorite books and resources about nonprofit fundraising?"

The team and I also leaned heavily on our board of directors and our newly formed advisory council—a non-governing group of super-volunteers lending their support and expertise to advise the staff and the board. We recruited experts in areas we needed support. Our first cohort of board members and council members were entrepreneurs themselves, helping us through the early stages of starting the museum. For the next cohort, we recruited based on our needs as we sought to grow: expertise in marketing, business development, public relations, and strategy. What we lacked in expertise, we made up for by recruiting an expert to advise us. This was a group I could meet with, call, or send an email to with any question at any time. Learning from the board and council allowed us to accelerate finding product-market fit, monetization, and financial stability—their advice was critical to every aspect of our business.

We also engaged experts as consultants, both paid and pro bono—we had very little budget for this in the beginning, but that grew over time. In our online community and within our board and council, we would simply ask for help, and if someone in that group could help, great. If not, they usually had a contact for an expert we could talk to or perhaps hire. This happened for accounting. I was learning about finance and accounting in graduate school, but this was something I was still very weak in. We got a connection to an accountant who was just starting his own practice, Adam Dworkin. We hired him for a fraction of what he would eventually charge clients—it helped that we were a small nonprofit.

While that nonprofit card comes in handy from time to time, I'd caution anyone from starting a nonprofit versus a for-profit, but that's a separate book. Adam helped get us set up on Quickbooks and advised us on organizing our already mounting pile of receipts. Later, we got a ton of pro bono tax preparation and filing help. Derek's girlfriend Jenna was contracting at a very small accounting firm called DMC Accounting + Technology, doing some graphic and web design. When she told her boss Doris Cahill that the museum was in dire need of tax prep help, she generously offered to meet with Derek and me to help us get into compliance with the IRS.

Formal education was also critical for me in my quest to learn everything it would take to make Design Museum Boston a success. I had to convince myself that this future was a real possibility. I knew I could start something—I'd done that before—but I knew I didn't have the business knowledge I needed to ensure its success. I was becoming an expert in design, and I had raw entrepreneurial talent, but I wanted to get this right. I wanted to learn how to manage and grow a business.

The same month Derek and I incorporated Design Museum Boston, August 2009, I started the evening MBA program at Babson College. Babson was known as the number one business school for entrepreneurship, and I wanted to learn how to be a successful entrepreneur so I could do justice to the big idea of starting a museum. It was brutal working all day at my corporate job and then jumping into classes from 6 to 9 pm, but the program was amazing. I was learning a ton about how businesses work: organizational behavior, financial accounting, entrepreneurial strategy, statistics, and more. It was one of the hardest things I've ever done, but it was worth it to get the formal training in a field that would help my business thrive.

The program at Babson was all about entrepreneurship, and when my professors learned I was actually starting a new business, they were thrilled and allowed me to use the Design Museum on many of my projects. In my organizational behavior class, I mapped out our community strategy from structuring the board of directors to what an ideal staff organization chart could look like in order for us to grow. In my information technology course, I developed a long-term IT strategy, looking at each area of the business from ticket sales for events, donations from supporters, project management for the team, etc. I still pull up that IT strategy thirteen years later as a guide for how we use technology at the museum to support the business.

In my entrepreneurial finance course, my amazing professor, Leslie Charm, noticed I was completely disinterested in venture capital and term sheets—that just didn't apply to starting and running a nonprofit. He sat me down and asked what would be helpful in the context of major funding for my fledgling nonprofit business. From talking to some of the development experts around Boston, I learned about capital campaigns as a way to raise large amounts of money in support of an organization. Traditionally, capital campaigns fund new capital purchases, hence the name—primarily

buildings, but also things like vehicles or important equipment
—but I wanted to study what a capital campaign could look
like for an organization that didn't have aspirations for a
building and didn't require many capital assets. Professor
Charm gave me the green light, and I used the opportunity to
develop a fundraising campaign strategy that, again, I still
refer back to a decade later—that coursework formed the
foundation for our fundraising approach.

Whether it was reading books, asking questions of experts,
hiring consultants, or learning in the classroom, I was applying
everything I was learning to my business in real time. That was
the key. It wasn't hypothetical. I learned about an accounting
concept in class in the evening, and the next morning, I looked
at our books and our accounting processes in a completely
different light. I learned about growth strategies at night, and
in the morning, crafted real scaling ideas for the Design
Museum and shared them with the team. Trying and doing
was so important in quickly solidifying the knowledge and
making it part of my toolkit for running the museum. Learn,
try, do, learn, try, do, repeat, repeat, repeat.

Humans think and learn in so many different ways—we all
process and retain information differently. In Howard
Gardner's 1983 book *Frames of Mind*, he outlined his theory of
multiple intelligences. It's a psychological theory that proposes
that rather than a single, general intelligence, people have
several different types of intelligence. According to Gardner,
traditional definitions of intelligence are based on cognitive
abilities such as memory, problem-solving, and logic—but to
him, this is too narrow. He proposed there are multiple human

intelligences that are distinct but interact with each other. The theory includes eight intelligences:

- Linguistic intelligence: the ability to use language effectively, including speaking, writing, and reading
- Logical-mathematical intelligence: the ability to reason, calculate, and think logically
- Spatial intelligence: the ability to perceive and manipulate visual and spatial information
- Musical intelligence: the ability to create, understand, and appreciate music
- Bodily-kinesthetic intelligence: the ability to control one's body movements and coordination
- Interpersonal intelligence: the ability to understand and interact with others
- Intrapersonal intelligence: the ability to understand one's own emotions and thoughts
- Naturalistic intelligence: the ability to understand and appreciate the natural world.[5]

I first came across Gardner's theory in an article in Design Museum Magazine, written by Stefanie Friedhoff, where she profiles a new type of school, The Acera School, founded by Courtney Dickinson. Dickenson utilized the theory of multiple intelligences to design a school and curriculum that catered to all eight intelligences rather than traditional schools which mainly focus on Linguistic and Logical-mathematical. She believes that by broadening the range of learning approaches, she could reach more kids, and those kids could therefore reach their full potential.[6] I think about Gardner's theory quite

---

[5] Howard Gardner & Thomas Hatch, "Multiple Intelligences Go to School: Educational Implications of the Theory of Multiple Intelligences," American Educational Research Association, November 1989, http://www.jstor.org/stable/1176460.

[6] Stefanie Friedhoff, "Learning While Doing at Acera," Design Museum Magazine, Winter 2017, https://designmuseumfoundation.org/learning-while-doing-at-acera/.

a bit because I believe education and learning are so critical for the creative entrepreneur. If we believe change is inevitable—change in society, economy, environment, and in ourselves—then we can either learn to respond to that change or better yet, learn in preparation for future change. I choose the latter.

An important part of my educational journey was and is learning how to harness all these types of intelligence toward real goals in my life. Let's look at another example: this book you're reading. I wanted to write this book for almost a decade, but I never took action. Finally, I realized, I need to learn about writing, understand how people do this, and try some things. I started by reading. I read countless books on how to write nonfiction, but the two books that actually cracked it for me had nothing to do with writing advice—they were about time and focus.

In *Four Thousand Weeks: Time Management for Mortals,* author Oliver Burkeman gets into how little time we really have on this earth—you guessed it, on average, only four thousand weeks—and how he spent his time worrying about and doing the wrong things, instead of focusing on what was important to him. He advocated for aligning your time with your life goals—writing this book was one of my life goals. In *Indistractable: How to Control Your Attention and Choose Your Life,* the author Nir Eyal advises readers on how to take their focus back from the world of social and technological distractions. The lesson of both books was clear: life is too short.

Reading to learn is just one facet for me. In addition to reading books about writing non-fiction and staying focused, I spoke with accomplished authors to learn about their writing process. It turns out the when and how are perhaps even more important than the what. I needed to set the conditions to be successful—the authors' advice was that I needed time and space. So I changed my behaviors and tried things. I set up a small folding desk and chair in our bedroom closet—just enough room for me to type. I started waking up before 5 am, before my young kids. And to remove any other distractions from technology, my wife bought me a Freewrite Traveler, basically a digital typewriter with no apps, no notifications, just a keyboard and a screen. At this moment, I'm at my little closet writing station with the lights off, typing away at 5:30 am. I cracked book writing by learning, trying, and doing.

———

How can you distribute your ignorance and learn while starting up your venture? Read all the books you can—it's not always obvious which books will help, so try to get recommendations. Google everything, read articles online, and listen to podcasts. Change your attitude from "I don't know how to do this," to "I don't know how to do this, yet." "Yet," is such a powerful word. Connect with experts and ask questions. If you're worried about looking silly (like me), find a lot of people, and ask each one a couple of questions. Trust me, by the end, you'll sound smarter and know more.

I believe every business needs an advisory group. Build one with people who complement your skillset, not a bunch of people who have the same skills and knowledge as you—that won't help. What expertise do you need that you don't have at your disposal? Write that down in one column, then in the next column, write people you know (or want to know) that have that expertise—then reach out, build relationships, and eventually, recruit them to your advisory group.

Take classes. You can go (or go back) to school as I did, or there is a wealth of educational experiences available online and in your community. Skillshare, General Assembly, Lynda.com, MasterClass—the Internet is full of accessible courses that can level up your knowledge in a variety of fields. Again, identify what you need to learn, and then deliberately seek out more formalized experiences where you can learn from experts in a way that suits your learning style.

Figure out the time, space, and tools it will take to actually try out what you're learning while you're learning it. What's the point of all this knowledge gathering if you don't apply it to your business? Try things out, test the ideas you're taking in, and solidify your new expertise in real time. It's impossible and totally okay not to know everything it takes to launch and run your business—as long as you're willing to learn, ask questions, and problem-solve. We are living in the easiest time in all of human history to start something because of the sheer amount of information available. Knowledge is democratized via the Internet, and social media makes it easier than ever to reach out to almost anyone and learn from their experience. Your most important skill as a founder is the ability to figure things out. You don't need to do that alone, but you do need to take responsibility for your learning journey.

Distributing my ignorance—whether at Bose in the corporate environment, or in my work in the nonprofit community in Boston, allowed me to build a ton of relationships in a short amount of time. I found at Bose that asking people questions makes them feel like experts, and people like feeling like experts. What I was really doing was building trust. A strange thing happened at Bose. As I was distributing my ignorance—connecting with people all over the company—I suddenly found myself engaged in a wide array of interesting projects. People started recruiting me because I built trust, and perhaps in the end, I became an expert in their eyes.

CHAPTER 7

Incremental Risk Mitigation

One step at a time.

"It's a myth that entrepreneurs are risk-takers. In fact, they're optionality-maximizers."

— Paras Chopra, entrepreneur

I was working full-time at Bose as an industrial designer, running the local Industrial Designers Society of America chapter, teaching undergraduate design courses at Wentworth Institute of Technology at night, earning my MBA at Babson on the other nights, and working on Design Museum Boston. It was a lot at once. Something had to give if the museum was going to get the attention it needed and grow into what I dreamed it could be.

In 2008, there was a round of layoffs at Bose that made me question just how stable a corporate job was. My job survived, but the experience made me want to take control of my own destiny. But was I ready to take the leap out of full-time employment? Did it really have to be such a big, scary leap?

Jason Schupbach made good on his offer at the bar across from Boston City Hall. He arranged a meeting for us with the business development team within the Boston Redevelopment Authority (BRA). In the afternoon on January 29, 2010, Derek and I took the elevator to the top floor of City Hall to meet with Randi Lathrop, Deputy Director of Community Planning, and Kristin Phelan, Assistant Director of Press & Marketing, in a little conference room in the BRA's offices. Both were full of energy—Randi was effervescent as she talked about arts and culture in Boston and how it could lead to economic development. She reminded me a bit of Mrs. Claus if Mrs. Claus worked in city government. She was full of ideas and endlessly optimistic. Kristin was young and full of ideas as well—she wanted to make Boston the best city it could be. We loved them both immediately. And they were both incredibly enthusiastic about the vision for Design Museum Boston. After hearing our story, they immediately asked how they could help.

Derek and I went on to talk about how inspired we were by the *Boston Art Windows* in Downtown Crossing—which Randi loved because the program was her brainchild. We wanted to expand on that and pop up our first design exhibition in one of the empty storefronts in Downtown Crossing. The exhibition would be called *Creative Capital: Designed in Boston* and would feature Boston-based designers across various design fields, showcasing their stories and their work. There was one empty space, in particular, we were interested in. It was the old Barnes & Noble bookstore in the heart of Downtown

Crossing, Boston's downtown business and retail district. The building had a beautiful sweeping facade, almost like an old cinema. As big readers, Derek and I spent a lot of time at that bookstore over the years, and sadly, it had closed. We wanted to turn it into Design Museum Boston for a few months and make a big splash in the city.

Randi was very into the idea. This was something that would bring life to Downtown Crossing during the devastating economic downturn. She loved the notion of using art to bring people together. She pledged her support and promised to connect us with a handful of building owners in Downtown Crossing whom she thought might be open to the idea, including the owner of the old Barnes & Noble space. We left that meeting on cloud nine—something was going to happen, and the City of Boston was behind us!

Over the next few weeks, Randi introduced us to a handful of building owners in Downtown Crossing. We had a few email exchanges and phone calls, but they didn't go so well. None of the owners understood what we were trying to do, and frankly, we were so early-stage, we couldn't meet their demands. It was one thing to hang art in their windows, but it was another to actually occupy the space and welcome people in. In most cases, that was going to require an expensive lease with a one-year minimum commitment—we were thinking only a few months, and we had almost no money. We were hoping to activate the space in exchange for free space. For the owners looking to lease their empty spaces, that wasn't enough. They wanted a tenant. They also all required insurance—we had no money and no insurance. Some of the folks we talked to on the phone openly laughed at our idea and our proposal. So much for that—we were too new and unestablished.

One night, Derek and I found ourselves walking through Downtown Crossing on Washington Street. After all the rejections, we were just sort of walking aimlessly, not even talking—which was weird for us—until we reached the Barnes & Noble building. We stopped to gaze at the empty facade. We were so close. It was right there, empty, but it wasn't going to happen. All of a sudden, someone grabbed us both from behind—we went into that fight-or-flight mode, thinking we were about to get mugged. But no, it was Mrs. Claus: Randi Lathrop. Derek kept her and Kristin in the loop throughout our space-seeking process, so Randi knew we were feeling dejected. Every connection they made for us failed to catalyze our first exhibition space opportunity. Seeing us stare up at that empty building that night, I know she felt for us. She suggested we meet up again at City Hall in the next couple of weeks and talk about options—she said there had to be a space we could pop up in.

So we found ourselves back at City Hall in the same little conference room with Randi and Kristin at the BRA—tails between our legs. Randi and Kristin brainstormed a bit, talking through options; neither Derek nor I had much to add to the conversation, but it was always fun to watch these two run through ideas at such a rapid rate. Their idea generation slowly ramped down. There just weren't any good options beyond who Randi had already connected us with. And then Randi just blurted it out, "Why don't you just have the exhibition here!" That perked us right up. An exhibition at Boston City Hall would be incredible. Boston was the Creative Capital of Massachusetts and New England, and City Hall was at the heart of the city. Countless people visit the building on a daily basis to do everything from paying parking tickets to getting married—the BRA in particular was a highly trafficked part of the building. Every building owner, real estate developer, and architecture firm had to present their proposals at the BRA to get approvals. It was perfect. Randi was a genius and our savior.

We got to work immediately preparing a concept design with our exhibition design friend, Brandon Bird, who generously volunteered and donated his expertise. We started curating the content for the show. As we got into it, one thing was very apparent: the launch party may have been our first big event, but this was going to be our real public debut and a proof of concept for our pop-up museum idea. I also realized that doing this as a side project wasn't going to work anymore. There was just too much to do to only be doing it at night and on the weekends. Between Derek and me, at least one of us needed to focus on the Design Museum much more, and that meant making a big change.

———

When you think of entrepreneurs founding startups, you might think, like I once did, about people breaking off all past responsibilities and taking a leap to risk it all for the chance to grow their business. For that notion to exist, there must at least be a sliver of truth to it. Or maybe it's just the story we tell ourselves after we gloss over the gory details. Taking a giant risky leap isn't the only way, and it certainly wasn't my way. There was no doubt that the museum needed more of our time, but I couldn't drop everything to pursue such a risky idea. I wasn't independently wealthy, the museum wasn't pulling in much money—we did have some folks making small donations via the website and a few design firms were sponsoring us, but it was nowhere near enough. I had bills to pay and needed food to live. The Design Museum idea was so important to me, but I just couldn't risk my entire financial well-being on it. My corporate design job gave me a pretty nice paycheck and wonderful benefits—if I left my job to pursue my startup, I'd be leaving amazing health insurance, a 401k with matching, and Bose even had a pension at that time, which I was super close to becoming fully vested in. If I left, I'd be saying goodbye to the pension, and what's worse, the Commonwealth of Massachusetts was requiring people to retain health insurance, so I would have to pay out of my own pocket.

It was because of our full-time jobs that Derek and I didn't need to focus on revenue at the museum. We could build our community, create our experiences, and establish the brand without worrying about where the next dollar was going to come from. But we were working morning, noon, and night on the museum. There was no free time, no breaks. We were burning vacation days in order to miss work and take meetings in Boston with partners and supporters. Even during my breaks at the office, I was thinking about and working on the museum, answering emails, and making plans. I always gave 100% at my job, and giving 90% felt strange. Working full-time, volunteering for the IDSA, teaching at night, getting my MBA, and running this fledgling startup—all at the same time —was wearing thin. How long could I juggle all of this? I was fine spending and risking my free time to try to make something happen, but this was getting ridiculous. And the *Creative Capital* exhibition at Boston City Hall was a very real opportunity that required a lot more dedicated time. Something had to give.

As I often did, I got out a sheet of paper with two columns and started writing and analyzing. I put my revenue from Bose and teaching in one column and my monthly expenses in the other. I realized I could reduce my expenses and live on less, but when it got down to it, I still needed some predictable money coming in. Besides time and money, I also really needed more flexibility and proximity to Boston to push the museum forward. Both Derek and I were working corporate jobs west of Boston in Framingham, MA—not the most convenient place when you want to meet with folks in downtown Boston. If I was going to leave my corporate job, I'd need to replace that income with something, ideally something flexible and in Boston. I figured if I could teach more classes and freelance for a few clients, I could make it happen. And teaching more classes could be possible if I wasn't constrained to only teaching at night. I was pretty confident that my network of design companies could yield a few freelancing side gigs. We were in a gig economy after all—the recession had businesses worried about hiring full-time workers, but they still needed the work to get done. Enter the gig workers—I could be that.

Teaching more seemed essential for me to be able to leave my corporate job. It was predictable revenue, and honestly, once I created a syllabus and the projects for a course, it didn't take a lot of my cognitive energy—being in the classroom felt easy to me—so I had some brain power left over for the museum. When I reached out to my manager at Wentworth Institute of Technology, he said that, unfortunately, I was already teaching the maximum number of courses they allowed for adjunct professors. I immediately called Jamie Read at MassArt—conveniently located right across from Wentworth in Boston. Jamie said he'd love for me to teach at MassArt, but they didn't have any courses available. I couldn't balance my equation without teaching more classes. If I didn't secure more income from teaching, I couldn't leave my job, and if I couldn't leave my job, I definitely couldn't freelance. And if I couldn't do either, I couldn't focus on the museum and develop our proof of concept exhibition. I was stuck.

It was July 2010, and Nicole and I were visiting my parents in Erie, Pennsylvania, for the July 4th holiday. On the drive back to Boston, we got into how I could possibly leave my job to spend more time on the Design Museum. Nicole had already given her notice at the EPA in order to go to graduate school for ceramics. Her manager offered to convert her to part-time since there was a hiring freeze, and they needed the support. Nicole would keep one foot in her government job, the other in the world of ceramics—at least till she could graduate and establish her studio. But as Nicole and I talked on that eight-hour drive, we just couldn't square it for me. I arrived back at our place feeling hopeless. Then my phone rang. It was Jamie Read from MassArt sounding sad—he went on to tell me that one of their long-time professors passed away over the weekend, and he was scrambling to get his classes covered with the semester starting in August. He asked if I could commit to teaching two classes. I probably sounded way too enthusiastic after just hearing about someone's passing, but I immediately shouted, "Yes! Sign me up!"

That was Monday. That Friday, I gave my two-week notice at Bose. The conversation with my boss, Michael Laude, was one of the hardest conversations I've ever had. I loved my job and the people I worked with. We had been through so much together and were recognized as one of the best design teams in the world—you don't just up and leave that. Mike believed in me and took a chance on me when I was twenty years old, when I had no business working with such an amazing group of designers. Mike and the rest of the team—Rich Carbone,

Seth Green, Julie Tierney, Carl Price, Dave Pitcher, and more
—taught me so much.

When I told Mike I was moving on, I still didn't have the
confidence to say it was to start a nonprofit museum. I told
him it was to focus on my master's in business. He was proud,
but I could tell he was sad to lose me—plus, like the EPA, Bose
also had a hiring freeze. I offhandedly mentioned Nicole also
left her job to pursue a master's degree and that her boss
offered to keep her on for a few days a week. Mike seized on
that and asked if I would consider contracting a couple of
days a week while I was in school. Bose would become my
freelance client. With teaching and freelancing coming
together, things were falling into place because of the amazing
community around me.

———————

I couldn't just leave my job outright with nothing to support
myself. The idea here was to step up or increase my risk
gradually so I could incrementally mitigate it—not leave
everything to pursue a super risky idea—but to slowly,
deliberately walk toward more risk, while developing the
museum into something more established. Picture two
opposing flights of stairs, pressed right next to each other, but
in opposite directions—the steps cross in the middle. At the
top set of stairs are economic stability and certainty. At the
bottom of each flight is lava—just kidding—it's worse:
financial risk, uncertainty, and doom. My plan was not to
jump into the risk lava. That's the entrepreneurship myth our
society popularizes as the only way. I would walk down one
step at a time toward the risk, while simultaneously building
that other flight of stairs next to me. That flight was the

Design Museum, and as I built it, it would become a real entity that could support full-time employees. As I walked down toward uncertainty, at some point—when the museum was ready—I would hop over to the other staircase and walk back up toward stability. You can do this too.

I loved my job at Bose, and I still miss it sometimes. Don't leave your full-time job until you have a plan. Use your paycheck as seed capital for your entrepreneurial adventure. The drive home on my last day as a corporate designer felt glorious instead of terrifying because I had a plan. That summer, I ended my term as chair of IDSA Boston, stopped working full-time, started freelancing, taught at two colleges, pursued my MBA, and most importantly, focused much more on building Design Museum Boston. As usual, my community made this possible. Over the years, I freelanced for Bose, for Jamie at his design firm Redfish, and Derek even hired me to freelance at Philips. My freelance business and teaching gave me confidence that I had a fallback plan. I had multiple fallback plans. If the museum failed, I could teach, I could continue freelancing, or I could get another job—maybe right back at Bose if I wanted.

What can you do to create more time and space to work on your startup? Your venture is likely already a side hustle, and that's great! Do you want it to be more? If you can reduce your living expenses and ramp up revenue quickly, your staircase might have just one step—go for it. The Design Museum wasn't a sure thing, though. Think about other ways you can earn income, less risky ways that don't require you to sit in an office for 40-50 hours per week. Maybe you can teach, consult, or get a part-time job that leaves you with enough cognitive capacity at the end of the day that you can refocus on the real prize: your startup. Perhaps your part-time job is related to your startup idea, so you're earning a living and gaining experience—win-win. It might be tempting, and it might be what society dictates for the "risk-taking entrepreneur," but you do not need to take a giant leap into your startup. As excited as you are about it, it's okay to take baby steps. Get creative with how you augment your time and how you balance your income and expenses, and gradually, you can make it work. Balancing a million things wasn't sustainable long-term for me, and I'm betting it's not possible for you. But work at it, come up with a plan, and be deliberate about slowly, incrementally mitigating your risk.

———

With more time and flexibility and access to the city, I was able to put a lot more of my effort into developing the museum. I was constantly meeting with potential partners and supporters, and in between designing and curating the *Creative Capital* exhibition for City Hall, I was still working constantly. That summer, everyone in my family met in Las Vegas for a much-needed family vacation. I was by the pool every day with my laptop designing the wall panels for *Creative Capital.* We curated twelve amazing case studies of design happening in Boston, labeled and organized by various design fields. We envisioned the exhibition as the first course in an ongoing public design curriculum. Creative Capital was *Intro to Design 101* featuring incredible creative work happening in Boston. The exhibit included industrial design work ELEVEN did to create Oxo's beautiful line of bar tools and tableware, the fashion design of *Project Runway* finalist Maya Luz, Korn Design's rebranding of the Boston Ballet, Boston City Hall itself as our example of local architecture, and more.

We curated and designed a really cool exhibition—the only problem was we had no idea how we were going to actually make it real. Once again, our community came to our aid. We were so transparent about what we were doing with the museum at all times. When we received approval to produce an exhibition at City Hall, we posted the great news on our social network, designingamuseum.org. Everyone knew what we were working on and what our needs were.

One day, I got a call from a guy named Rich Dooley. He was in business development at AIR Graphics, a local printing company, and was a member of our online community. After introducing himself and letting me know how excited he was about our new museum, he asked, "How the heck are you going to print this exhibition for City Hall?" I said that I hadn't quite figured that out yet. He replied, saying that AIR Graphics would love to print the show pro bono in exchange for sponsorship visibility. Half of our problem was solved. Then, as if lightning could strike twice, it did. I received an email from Bob Russo at VDA Productions, a local fabricator and experience design company that worked with many museums in the area. Bob asked me if we needed help fabricating and installing the exhibition—yes, we most certainly did. We built a partnership, and they fabricated the entire exhibition for free as another sponsor of the program. *Creative Capital* wouldn't have happened without them. Was I that lucky? Or did cultivating a community create luck for the Design Museum?

Together with AIR Graphics, VDA, Derek, myself, our volunteers, and a ton of help from Kristin Phelan, we installed *Creative Capital: Designed in Boston* at Boston City Hall and opened it to the public in October 2010. We held an epic opening reception in December. Derek borrowed about

Giving a tour of Creative Capital to a group of students from Madison High School, Boston

$200,000 worth of LED lighting from his company and proceeded to install it around and within City Hall. When our guests walked across City Hall Plaza toward the building, they were met with a shifting rainbow light show—the brutalist City Hall truly never looked that good. This was our moment.

When you entered City Hall, you entered onto the third floor. Again, you were met with beautiful colored lighting that transformed the already tall ceilings and geometric architecture into something magical. There was huge red signage welcoming you to Design Museum Boston and *Creative Capital.* Up the wide grand brick staircase to the main landing, and you arrived at the party. We had food and live music—our whole community was there. Once again, I had my supportive family there. My sister Kate flew in from Atlanta to help out, and Nicole was there too, along with the entire Design Museum volunteer squad and our board of directors.

To enter the main exhibition area, you took the elevator to the top floor of City Hall. Right off the elevator, the main wall was covered in a huge red fabric banner with our exhibition branding, *Creative Capital: Designed in Boston,* emblazoned over a map of New England and a star over Boston which also doubled as the dot over the *I* in the word *Capital*—a quintessential Derek design touch. That red banner took up your entire view—you weren't in City Hall anymore. You were at the Design Museum.

We learned from our research on Boston City Hall's architecture that the interior concrete walls were formed using slats of wood—each about four inches wide—to create the volumes the concrete was poured into. You could still see the impressions of those wooden slats embossed in the concrete walls. We brought some of that back and created a physical undulating pattern of wooden slats behind the exhibition panels. The wood elements, the red on the interior walls, the rich imagery of the exhibition panels, and the artifacts on pedestals truly transformed the space from a cold concrete interior to a modern, warm, welcoming museum. There was also so much great info on the panels, and it was great to have architectural models and real designed artifacts in the space. Each panel had a QR code that folks could scan with their phone which took them to our website and a landing page for each project, with more information, videos, and a link to join our community.

Standing in the beautiful pop-up exhibition we created, I couldn't help but think, *if we can transform Boston City Hall, we can transform any space into the Design Museum.* Thanks to a lot of volunteers and partners, and to the fact that I created time and space in my life to dedicate to the museum, we did it. Four years after the initial kernel of the idea, eighteen months after

Derek and I officially incorporated Design Museum Boston, and nine months after our launch party, we were standing in our proof of concept.

CHAPTER 8

Early Amplified Presence

Look good, look real.

"Presentation is everything."
— Wendy Aquillano, my mom

If you were at that Boston City Hall exhibition opening reception, you were, for all intents and purposes, at a real, established museum—thanks to good design and attention to detail. In reality, we were still a small group of volunteers with about $2,000 in the bank. Thanks to our presentation, we looked bigger than we actually were. We had our Boston debut, and now it was time to introduce ourselves to the world. Derek had an idea that would reshape our brand into one of our most important assets.

I mentioned Earthworks Lawncare earlier, the lawn-mowing and landscaping business I had with my brother Steve. Our

parents wanted us to work, but we valued our independence—
we didn't want a part-time job. We wanted to control our time.
We started with a few lawns in the neighborhood, mostly folks
who knew our parents. But we earned enough to invest in a
small tractor and some other equipment. We found pretty
quickly that word of mouth was key. Our new customer
acquisition usually went something like this: someone would be
planning to go on vacation and needed someone to take care
of their lawn while they were away. They'd ask their neighbor
or friends for recommendations, and they'd learn about these
two kids who were very inexpensive and did a nice job. They
would call our parents, and we'd set up a meeting where they'd
tell us they were going to be away for the next couple of weeks
and needed their lawn mowed and generally kept up while
they were gone. We would mow their lawn, do an awesome
job, and only charge $20 or $40. When they came back they'd
be so happy (and hooked on inexpensive lawn care) that they'd
call us again to take care of their lawn on a weekly basis.

We saw this pattern play out over and over again. Steve
and I wanted more lawns and more money, so we came up
with an idea. Folks in our neighborhood were still hiring
professional lawn care services and paying a lot more. We
wanted to look like one of those services as much as possible.
Looking like the competition could shield the fact that we were
a pair of young teenagers long enough for us to get our foot in
the door with new customers, hit them with our low price, and
undercut the competition. I sat down at our Gateway 2000
computer with a crude image editor and started working on a
name and a logo for us. Steve and I came up with Earthworks
Lawncare, and I designed a logo that looked like a simple
green tree in a white circle. It looked like what the professional
lawn companies had on the sides of their trucks—it looked

real. To boost our customer acquisition, we wanted to make it easier for folks to call us when they needed a one-off lawn service—basically, we wanted to accelerate them finding us versus having to ask around for ideas.

Keep in mind, this was the early 90s. The Internet was just barely a thing, and phone numbers were still only seven digits. Our refrigerator had a few magnets from local services we used like a plumber, a bakery, and a few others. They were like little ads people willingly displayed in their own homes. We could do this. Back in my image editing software, I placed our white circle with the tree logo in it on a field of freshly mowed grass with "Earthworks Lawncare" written across the top and our home phone number across the bottom. My mom found packs of self-adhesive magnetic sheets at the local office supply store. We printed sheets of the branded grassy rectangles, adhered them to the magnet sheets, and cut out each magnet with an X-acto knife. The result looked like all the other refrigerator magnet ads we had in the kitchen. It looked professional. We also printed the logo on some envelopes and distributed the magnets to all the houses in our neighborhood. Then we sat back from our DIY marketing effort and waited for the calls to come in. And, boy, did folks call.

———

Steve and I were branding our entrepreneurial venture. The word *brand* comes from Old Norse, the language from which present-day Scandinavian languages derive. *Brand* meant "a piece of burning wood." In the mid-14th century, *brand* evolved to mean "mark permanently with a hot iron," and in the 17th century, it referred to a mark of ownership. Of course, the act of branding pre-dates the actual word by thousands of years. Four to five thousand years ago, ancient potters and stone masons marked their wares and materials with different engravings to denote who made what.[7] I always think about a family's coat of arms in the Middle Ages. Brand became a symbol or group of symbols that represented something, a person, a family, or an organization. But it's even more than that. It's also memories. Brands live inside our minds with inputs across all five senses.

When you go to the hardware store to buy a hammer, you're seeing brands in the wild. Marketing experts estimate that in the United States, we're exposed to 4,000 to 10,000 brand messages per day.[8] Brands manifest as touch points. The product itself, the hammer, is the ultimate manifestation of the brand, with its color, materials, form, weight, smell—then there's the packaging color, graphics, and logo. But there's something else: your memory of working in your grandfather's workshop and the tools he had. You have a history that shapes your feeling for what makes a good hammer. You remember hammering a nail into a block of wood for the first time and whacking your thumb.

All your memories about hammers and what, where, how, and with whom you've used them shape your desire—and it's what savvy designers and marketers think about when creating a brand and designing a hammer. They want to evoke those feelings to get you to choose their brand. Maybe like Stanley, they want to own a color, yellow. Your Dad used Stanley tools, which means tools are yellow, so you're buying a Stanley hammer, or at least one with a yellow grip. Maybe it's

---

[7] Taylor Holland, "What Is Branding? A Brief History," Skyword, August 11, 2017, https://www.skyword.com/contentstandard/branding-brief-history/.

[8] Ron Marshall, "How Many Ads Do You See in One Day?," Red Crow Marketing, September 10, 2015, https://www.redcrowmarketing.com/blog/many-ads-see-one-day/.

something else, a wooden handle or something heavy and well-built that evokes a sense of quality that matches your feelings and memories. It's all brand.

Besides our people, our brand is our most important asset. Without a physical museum building, it is the strongest signal we have. It's what draws people to us. The same is true for your business. Forget "don't judge a book by its cover." Humans do it constantly. We make decisions on our engagement with everything from hammers to doctors based on the manifestations of their brand across the touch points with which we interact. We associate the brand with the feeling we get from the interaction. Scientists have shown that the anticipation of interaction is more powerful than the actual act of partaking. Neuroscientist Read Montague showed that merely seeing the Coca-Cola brand was enough to activate the brain's pleasure centers in the prefrontal cortex, producing the feel-good hormone, dopamine—no sip required. Dopamine is responsible for the feeling of pleasure and excitement associated with anticipation. It is released in our brain even when we only imagine and anticipate an event or outcome. Brand creates those connections in our brains and builds anticipation for feelings and things we want.[9]

Because of my mom's mantra of "presentation is everything," with any business I've started—whether it was Earthworks Lawncare or Design Museum Everywhere—I've sought to use branding to look bigger, and more established, than an early-stage startup. It works because not only do our brains make connections between specific brands and feelings of quality and anticipation, but we build connections around *types* of brands. If your brand can connect at that level, you

---

[9] Douglas Van Praet, "How Brands Addict Us," Psychology Today, September 24, 2017, https://www.psychologytoday.com/us/blog/unconscious-branding/201709/how-brands-addict-us/.

become associated with the same feelings and desires as other high-quality brands. You do this through design and good, thoughtful presentations of your brand so that folks don't see you as a nascent venture with no money and nothing yet to offer. They see you from the start as they see comparable, more established businesses in the marketplace.

I created the first Design Museum visual brand by emulating other Boston-based museums: the Museum of Fine Arts; the Museum of Science, Boston; the Institute for Contemporary Art. You need to start with something and get rolling. The logo I came up with at the start was a simple line of all-capitalized text in red, using a well-known typeface, Helvetica Neue. "Design Museum" was bold text and "Boston" was regular. It was nothing special, designed as a placeholder until we could spend the time to do something befitting our vision for the museum. It worked for starting up because it used similar font, color, and imagery as other museums in the Boston area that people knew. But we needed a brand that people recognized and would last as an authentic manifestation of our vision.

———————

Derek had a friend at a Boston-based, world-renowned design firm called Continuum. Continuum is probably best known for designing products like the first Reebok Pump sneaker and the first Swiffer mop. But they had a new brand design team that they created to offer branding services to clients. Derek's pal John Magnifico was on the team, and they were scheming on a collaboration between Continuum and Design Museum Boston. They had a very interesting idea: Continuum would design the new Design Museum brand pro bono, and they'd do it in full view of the public, inviting feedback and critique from our audience online. This would give a lot of visibility to Continuum's new branding team and services, and give Design Museum a new brand and very public introduction to the broader design community. It was a win-win. But when Derek floated the idea to me, I must admit, I was scared.

Doing this work in full view of our new audience was risky. What if the work was terrible? Our relationship with Continuum, Derek's relationship with John, and the very public nature of the work meant that we'd probably have to use—and worse, pretend to like—whatever they came up with, even if we hated it. But Derek was right. This approach aligned with how we wanted to run the museum, always transparent and accessible. We wanted to show the design process that is so often hidden from view. This was the perfect opportunity to demonstrate to our audience that we were going to be transparent, participatory, and social about everything related to the museum.

Our board of directors loved the idea. Michael DiTullo was very active on a popular design website called core77.com, and he put us in contact with their editorial team. They loved the idea of being the platform for this project. We were in business. The Continuum team, comprised of John Magnifico, Bryant Ross, Peter Strutt, Will Thomas, Erik Lund, Samantha Allen, Beth Johnson, Leah Schwartz, and Alanna Fincke, got to work and created a weekly blog series on core77 called *Open for Branding* to chronicle their design process in real time.

The first post went up on core77 on July 28, 2010, to introduce the project. Design Museum Boston, a new, nomadic museum of design, would be the client, and the Continuum team would work on the brand identity, post their progress, and ask for folks' feedback at each critical moment. The response online was immediately enthusiastic and exciting. One commenter, Leeanne, posted, "Woah, this is a great idea. Has this ever been done before? I always love a good critique, and this is taking it to an interesting and exciting new level. I look forward to seeing the work and giving my 2 cents!" Another commenter, Rebecca, said, "Very interesting. Since one of the major hurdles of any redesign is how to get past the initial knee-jerk reactions, this approach not only provides transparency and inclusion but also education."

We were certainly the first nomadic design museum. How do you design a brand for a type of organization that has never existed before? It turns out there is a process for getting to the heart of an organization's ethos and vision to then design an authentic brand that evokes those values every time you see and interact with it. Everyone's design process is different but similar. Continuum's brand design process went something like this: first, learn. Ask probing questions and gather as much information about the organization as possible —its mission, approach, values, offerings, audience, trade secrets, and history. Once you've learned, you've created a space to work within that can be explored. You can ask yourself (and others) what images, words, and feelings are evoked by the organization. Designers then take that learning and exploration and develop concepts through sketching, prototyping, and good old-fashioned creative trial and error. They then narrow the concepts through feedback and critique, refining the best ideas to design the brand, then refining it further to deliver the brand identity to the client.

Continuum's first post on core77 launched the process: "Now that we've kicked off the project, where do we begin? If you jump right into design, you could go anywhere—the world of possibility is too big. First, you need to take a step back and establish some parameters. At Continuum, we develop thematic approaches to do this. By having a conversation around several approaches, we start to set boundaries to focus the creative direction." The project started with Derek and me visiting Continuum's modern brick offices in West Newton, MA. We had specific goals for the brand. We wanted to communicate that the museum is approachable, enthusiastic, and passionate about design impact. We needed the visual identity to align with our approach of transforming spaces into the museum using graphics and materials for our pop-up exhibitions and events. We wanted to educate the general public about design, not just talk about design to designers. And the identity needed to have flexibility so that we could apply it to exhibitions, merchandise, fundraising materials, our website, and more.

At the time, our organizational pillars were *educate, unite,* and *demonstrate.* After our initial meetings, the design team matched these with three themes they wanted to explore: *smart, dynamic,* and *bold.* The best part of the process was getting the community's feedback on core77.com. One commenter posted, "It's a transient museum; BOLD is key. It's key to grabbing instant attention and driving awareness as the museum travels about."

Each phase built on the last. John, Bryant, and the team started sketching concepts. The weeks of research, discussion, and idea generation started to gel into actual graphics on the page, visual manifestations of the brand. During the first graphics presentation, they showed Derek and me a huge range of concepts for possible graphic identities. The ideas and visuals were all over the place. I left that presentation sweating and freaking out. I didn't love any of the logomarks they were showing, and I complained to Derek that this was a

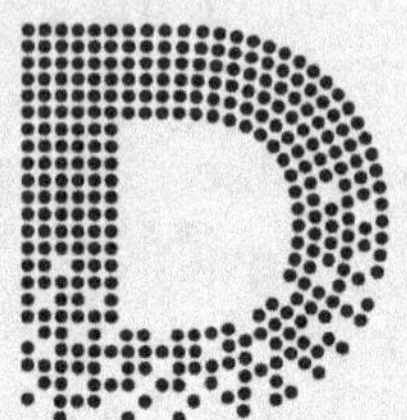

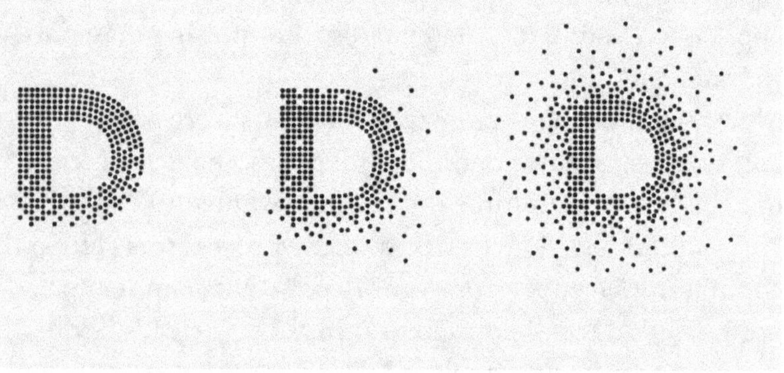

Design Museum main logo, and three states of the logomark, designed by Continuum

huge mistake. We were going to have to use something we hated because Continuum was doing this pro bono, and we were doing it all in full view of the public. Derek talked me down. He implored me to trust the design process and reminded me that we still had a long way to go.

The next round of refinement was so much better. The Continuum team knew what they were doing—I was sweating and worrying a lot less. The overwhelmingly positive direction from the surveys, comments, and from Derek and me was the

Design is Everywhere concept, with the scattered dots making up the letter "D." They created three states of the logo. Tight with the dots clearly forming a "D"; slightly dispersed, where some dots at the top and most at the bottom start moving away from the "D" form; and a very dispersed version where you can still barely make out that it's a letter "D," with the dots radiating out from the center—all together evoking the idea of people coming together and moving apart with each Design Museum pop-up installation, as well as symbolizing pins on a map that are ever-changing.

The audience on core77 agreed that the refinement from the previous stage was incredible. One person commented, "And somehow...it turns out perfect." We had our logo, our wordmark, and our color palette. Continuum delivered brand guidelines that specified each part of the brand with details on spacing, colors, and examples of expressions on business cards, letterhead, and our website. We successfully did an entire design project in full view of the public. The result proved we could be open and transparent as we educated the world about design. On core77, a commenter conveyed what many felt about the project, "Definitely an inspiration to be part of the process."

We talked to Continuum about hosting a special event where we would fully unveil and celebrate our collaboration and new brand. The design team loved the idea, and in January 2011, Continuum hosted a huge celebration with a giant exploded "D" projected onto the orange wall above their grand staircase, along with a full exhibition showcasing their design process. Folks could literally walk through the design process to get to the end result.

We made t-shirts and pins. This brand and museum were real, and people loved it. The Continuum team did it, and once again, we involved our community. I'll forever be indebted to the designers who gave their time and talents to make this happen, for believing in us enough to give us such an amazing gift—the gift that keeps on giving every time we utilize our brand.

You always want your brand—how you present your company—to look professional and to have that brand presentation evoke a business that's larger than you really are. That amplified presence will pull you to grow into what you want to be. Just like when Steve and I made a brand for our little landscaping business that evoked a professional lawn care service in the eyes of our customers, we established a brand for the Design Museum that we needed to grow into and live up to. You might not be able to get a firm like Continuum to donate hours and hours of their time for free to create your brand, but you can certainly hire a designer or a design team to create your brand—I highly recommend it. If you don't know any designers, you can reach out to folks online, or go to websites like 99designs or Fiverr, services that make it very easy to get a logo designed. Think of it as an investment in your future. You likely have a placeholder brand at this point that you did yourself, or maybe someone in your network did you a favor. That's great. But it's time to swing for the fences—don't cut corners, go through the full process to learn, explore, concept, design, and deliver a great brand for your business.

Create something that you, your team, and your customers will love. You don't have to do it in public, although I wish more organizations would. It made me sweat, but it was really fun to involve such a large number of people. It wouldn't hurt to involve some of your trusted community in the process, to get their feedback and direction. They'll feel good about being involved with your business, and you'll get those valuable additional insights. And then, of course, I highly recommend having a party to unveil the brand.

Remember, you're looking for reasons to celebrate with your community and ways to engage the press, and this is a very visual opportunity to do so. Don't be afraid to involve your customers in your brand across all five senses—make it real for them. I mentioned our brand is one of our most valuable assets. This brand is still in use to this day. It pulled us and continues to pull us into our future. Now thirteen years into this adventure, I still feel like it amplifies us beyond where we actually are as an organization. It pulls us toward a future state where we finally live up to this incredible visual identity.

CHAPTER 9

Respectful Opportunism

Everybody wins.

"It's through curiosity and looking at opportunities in new ways that we've always mapped our path."
— Michael Dell, Founder, Dell Technologies

With all the planning, coordination, blood, sweat, and tears leading up to our proof of concept exhibition, *Creative Capital,* at Boston City Hall, the Continuum brand project and launch, and all the community events and web content, we were on a nonstop sixteen-month sprint from August 2009 to January 2011, trying to figure out if there was an audience for our type of accessible design programming. It turns out there was, and now it was time to find or create more opportunities to connect with our audience. But Derek, the team, and I were all exhausted. We all put aside responsibilities and relationships to get the museum launched, and then in that moment of pause after the branch launch, all those previous responsibilities came flooding back in. We were laser-focused, eyes on the prize, up until this point—but what were we going to do next? We were tired and had no money, staff, or plan beyond this point. But this level of desperation had a way of turning every situation into an opportunity. So when Sam Montague, head of the Industrial Design department at Wentworth Institute of Technology approached us about co-teaching an exhibition design class during the summer semester, something clicked.

I was interested in teaching the class because I loved designing exhibitions, I really enjoyed teaching, and I needed the adjunct credit hours to keep paying my bills. I took two exhibition courses at RIT. In one, we picked a client or topic and designed an exhibition on paper—basically, a drawing class. We created a vision for what an exhibition could be and made a few drawings and renderings. It wasn't real, just purely conceptual. The other course was an independent study I did with another design student and a group of engineers to design, build, install, and test an exhibition about the earth's water cycle for the local science museum. We talked to folks at the museum, talked to kids and parents, studied the subject matter, designed concepts, built prototypes, and eventually built a full-scale, usable version of our exhibition. It was a giant jungle gym that started and ended in a big ball pit filled with blue plastic balls, symbolizing water molecules. Kids grabbed a ball and climbed up nets as evaporation, crawled through a tunnel as their water molecules condensed and became clouds, and then slid down the blue slide as they turned into rain, flowing back into the ball pit lake. It was real, and seeing the kids learn and play was glorious. I wanted that for my students at Wentworth, something real.

I went to Sam M. and Derek with the idea. We could teach the exhibition design course as one giant group project. Instead of designing random made-up exhibitions, the students would create a real exhibition for Design Museum Boston. They would do research, conceive the idea and theme, develop the content, get funding, design, build, market, and install their exhibition somewhere in the city. It would be a real project that would stretch their skills beyond just design and into business, marketing, operations, and more. Sam M. loved the idea. The students would have an amazing experience, the Design Museum would get its next exhibition, and Derek and I would be paid as instructors. Everybody would win! Derek and I collaborated on a rough syllabus, but really, he and I would simply act as studio managers, providing direction to the students and helping them create their exhibition.

The students took to it immediately. They started as a group, brainstorming exhibition ideas that they all cared about. From the beginning, I observed how much ownership they felt over this project. Even my students who normally struggled in studio classes were fully engaged in the process and participating in the team meetings. Derek and I set the framework and the mission for the Design Museum, and characterized our approach and audience for the students—from there, it was fully in their hands. They decided to curate an exhibition about the product life-cycle as it relates to environmental sustainability. I know many industrial design students struggle with the idea that the products they design will eventually end up in a landfill somewhere, and these students were no different. They wanted to educate themselves and the public on the complete life-cycle of various everyday products—water bottles, sneakers, cleaning products, cell phones—and offer an alternative that either extended the products' life cycles or allowed for proper reuse or recycling.

They called their exhibition *Retail: Retell. Recycle. Rethink.* Their work was amazing. They owned every step of the process by breaking into teams focused on content curation, design, fundraising, fabrication, and marketing. The marketing team identified a handful of venues around campus and around the city. They negotiated for and secured the grand concourse at the Prudential Center Mall as the venue, a space that saw thousands of people walk through it each day. The day after the Prudential Center venue was secured, one of our students, Haik, walked into our classroom with a scale model of the concourse. This wasn't something Derek or I assigned— he thought it would be a valuable tool in the final phase of the design process, so he built it. That was a powerful example of student ownership over the project.

The fundraising team opted to launch a Kickstarter crowdfunding campaign which raised $5,000 for the exhibition. Additionally, Wentworth donated thousands of dollars of materials for fabrication, and Derek and I were able to secure a few sponsorships, as well. In August 2011, in the middle of the night, the entire class loaded up a truck and installed the exhibition at Prudential Center. This included eight displays with graphics and artifacts as well as a massive 30-foot diameter version of the exploded "D" logo created on the floor with vinyl dots. The students made it happen, the exhibition looked spectacular, and the audience loved it. They planned an opening reception where you could easily see the immense pride the students had in their work. They never could have had this experience from just drawing exhibitions on paper, and the Design Museum never would have had a

Retail: Retell. Recycle. Rethink. exhibition at Prudential Center Mall, Boston, 2011.

new exhibition this soon after installing *Creative Capital* at Boston City Hall. Everybody won.

———

You need to create a lot of opportunities for your startup to survive and succeed. At this point in your journey, it's easy to have a one-track mind about your work and your venture. You can get tunnel vision, and your opportunity-making can steamroll others. The team at Design Museum was committed to an approach that was collaborative, and that unlocked opportunities for partnerships everywhere we went. Collaboration became the lifeblood of our little museum because, honestly, without a building, partnerships were all we had! We didn't have a building made of bricks. Our bricks were the relationships we were building every day. The desire to grow the Design Museum made us see opportunities for collaboration everywhere—some opportunities we created, some we sought out, and others came to us organically because we were so community-oriented and open to possibilities.

One of the first programs for the newly formed Design Industry Group of Massachusetts (DIGMA) was a one-day conference called *Design Means Business.* The team at DIGMA sought to gather folks from the business leadership, investment, and government worlds to showcase the impact of design on the bottom line. The conference would take place at Reebok's global corporate headquarters in Canton, Massachusetts, and DIGMA wanted a small exhibition program for the day. While folks were grabbing coffee in between presentations, they could read about and see examples of design projects where the work had a dramatic impact on the client's business. In addition to working on Design Museum Boston, I was advising DIGMA on various programmatic opportunities. So when I heard they wanted an exhibition at the *Design Means Business* conference, I quickly volunteered Derek and myself to produce a small show.

It was a great opportunity for us because DIGMA already curated all the content for the exhibition—our friend Stefane Barbeau was collecting business design case studies and had about a dozen ready to be turned into an exhibition. They also had a volunteer graphic designer engaged from Reebok with a creative direction that was pretty well set, based on their other conference branding and materials. Reebok also had an in-house print shop where the exhibition could be printed, and they had mobile displays on which we could mount the exhibition graphics and artifacts for showcasing everything. All the elements—content, design, displays—were accounted for.

What the DIGMA team needed was someone to own this part of the program, project manage, and bring it all together.

We saw it as an easy opportunity to test our mettle on exhibition development and get visibility amongst the design leaders and public officials who were slated to attend the conference. For their part, the DIGMA team likely could have pulled this off themselves, but I know they also wanted to see Design Museum Boston succeed. We were all part of the same community that was trying to elevate design in the state, and we were all willing to put in the time together.

In October 2010, we opened *Design Means Business* at Reebok headquarters. We mounted large graphic panels on the top half of both sides of Reebok's mobile displays, showing big images and text to tell the story of each design project. There was Zipcar, with their innovative car-sharing network; a story of Bank of America teaming up with IDEO to create the *Keep the Change* program to help people save money; Barbara Lynch, a successful local chef who partnered with local design firms on her restaurants to create uniquely designed and successful dining experiences. With the scale of the graphics and the multitude of artifacts, it was a great little exhibition. Attendees at the conference enjoyed it, and we got to prove ourselves again—we knew how to produce a great public exhibition on design.

———

One of the most important things to us in terms of introducing the public to design was making sure we showed the behind-the-scenes of the design process. We can trace this desire all the way back to the sketch on the back of the pizza box at MassArt. We wanted to show people all the creativity and intelligence that went into creating the places, things, and experiences they interacted with every day. What we found in our work curating the *Creative Capital* exhibition was that designers and design firms were pretty terrible at documenting their design process on various projects—so when we asked them to share images, assets, and stories about how they designed something, they didn't have much to share. Also, some design firms were pretty reluctant to share proprietary content that could tip their hand to the competition. Derek and I thought this was ridiculous, since, for the most part, every designer uses a similar design process, but we understood not wanting to share trade secrets.

None of this changed the fact that we really wanted to show the design process. We felt it was critical to the public understanding how design happens. Remember Michael DiTullo's music analogy: people can go see musicians make music at concerts, and in doing so, they tend to understand how music is produced and, therefore, appreciate high-quality music that they then listen to regularly. Design happens mostly behind closed doors, in secret—there are no design concerts. But what if there were? As we often did, we dreamed up concepts that were completely unrealistic but helped us set a vision for what we wanted to ultimately create. We envisioned a giant glass box, constructed in the middle of a public park. Inside, there would be designers doing their work in full view of the public. People could watch as designers did research, developed ideas, sketched, prototyped, and tested their prototypes. Basically, it was a design zoo. It was preposterous, but it got us thinking.

If folks were hesitant to share their design process, well, we were designers. We could do it ourselves. We did an entire brand design project in full view of the public, so we could do

Derek Cascio presenting concepts to the Smallbean team, 2010.

it again. This time, we wouldn't just show our audience the steps week to week, but we could also film everything and show folks the entire process. We just needed a project. Things often manifested for us in mysterious ways. As always, the community did not disappoint. Derek got connected to Sean Hewens and Ross Lohr, the founders of a small nonprofit called Smallbean, and they had a design problem. Smallbean was trying to provide technology-driven education to teens and adults in rural Tanzania. Their mission was to utilize mobile computer labs to empower people to document, preserve, and showcase endangered cultures around the world.

To do this, Smallbean hacked together some equipment to create a pop-up, solar-powered computer lab which could turn local schools or community buildings into technology education centers. It was a really neat idea. The problem was their hacked solution was in a suitcase, it looked like a bomb, and they had to bring it on planes. The "solar suitcase," as they called it, consisted of a classic clamshell suitcase—inside was a large battery, lots of red and black wires, and charging electronics that connected to solar panels that Sean and Ross would carry with them in other travel bags. They had to get this all through airport security and customs both ways on their journey to and from rural Africa. Sean would typically need to call ahead and explain what he was trying to bring to the airport—even so, getting through security was a nightmare each time. Plus, when they got to Tanzania, their hacked-together solution was prone to water and dust damage and often broke down during their limited time in each community.

Derek and I saw the design opportunity right away. We were both product designers, after all. We offered to recruit a volunteer team of experts, including ourselves, to redesign the solar suitcase and solar computer lab from the ground up, and deliver a fully productized solution to Smallbean. All the while, we would film and capture every minute of the design process for a series of videos and, ultimately, an exhibition of the process. Our collaboration with Continuum on our brand identity provided the framework. Now, we would do this at a much larger scale on something much more complicated that would make a huge impact on a local nonprofit and the people living over 7,000 miles away in Tanzania.

Derek expertly branded the program *Designing a Difference* and recruited his childhood friend, Tom Svenson, a talented filmmaker, to volunteer and capture the design process for the video series. Smallbean was thrilled to be the client and receive design services pro bono that would change and improve their whole operation—and we would get our wish to show the public the design process from beginning to end. Everyone was going to win once again.

We brought together an amazing volunteer design team including Anna Engstrom, a talented designer and project coordinator, who volunteered to manage our work with Smallbean. We also recruited two designers from Samsonite, knowing part of this project was going to be about luggage to contain the solar computer lab components. Samsonite's design director Jason Gifford and another designer from their team, Tony Quartarone, who was our friend from college, joined the team. We also successfully pitched Samsonite to fund the project with a few thousand dollars and access to their prototyping facilities in Mansfield, MA. All the pieces were set.

Through a series of workshops with the Smallbean team and our volunteer team of designers, we went through the design process. We learned about the users and community stakeholders involved with education and the ins and outs of the computer labs in Tanzania. We couldn't travel to Africa, but we had Sean and Ross as our subject matter experts, and they showed us videos of interviews they did for the projects with folks on the ground. We learned a ton about how schools and community centers work in Tanzania, as well as the various players and community leaders. Derek pulled all these findings together into a journey map of how Smallbean typically collaborated with Tanzanian educators to pop up the solar-powered computer lab. That journey map provided us with the starting point—the current state of things—and we documented the challenges Sean and Ross faced with the technology products themselves from a travel and durability standpoint.

From there, the team went to work creating concepts to improve the overall experience for the stakeholders in Tanzania and the Smallbean team. The idea we developed allowed solar power to be used beyond the computer lab. Folks in the villages would be able to check out charged batteries as if they were checking books out of a library. So the solar suitcase would power the computer lab in the local school and also allow people to charge phones, use devices and appliances, and have electric lights at home.

Derek shined in this process. His designs and concept illustrations moved the project along super quickly. We visited the Samsonite design team a few times, and their prototype shop created physical samples of the bags that would hold the charging electronics, the laptops, and the batteries themselves. And we filmed everything. Tom was always there, helping to tell the story and share our progress. The videos were a hit in our community, who were sharing them widely on social media. In the end, we delivered a finished product solution, manufactured by Samsonite. It was a system of modular bags that solved a lot of the initial challenges and created some new opportunities for the Smallbean crew to serve folks on the ground. We got the chance to show the design process in full with videos and a digital exhibition on how design can make a big impact on people's lives.

—————

Through 2010 and 2011, between our launch party and our quarterly *UNITE* events, we were having a lot of community gatherings. But let's call them what they really were: a series of parties or networking events to bring the community together and introduce the Design Museum to large groups of people.

By the summer of 2011, I was feeling like we needed to infuse our events with more design thought leadership. In my previous activities, particularly as the chapter chair of the

Industrial Designers Society of America, I was accustomed to convening thought leaders and creating event experiences where people shared their ideas through talks, keynote presentations, panel discussions, workshops, and more. I wanted to bring that to the Design Museum and create accessible events for our growing community. Another amazing opportunity presented itself, and I pounced on it.

In 2008, Tina Roth-Eisenberg had an idea: she wanted to bring creative people together around design to share stories and ideas. She started a free event series in New York City called *CreativeMornings*. Every month on a Friday morning, Tina would host a new presenter who would give a short talk, 10-15 minutes, on a different topic, and they'd take questions from the audience. There was free coffee, and that was about it —simple. Folks attended to chat with fellow creatives, hear from an inspiring presenter, and then headed off to work (maybe a little late, but it was a Friday).

Rachael Chong speaking at one of the first CreativeMornings Boston events, 2011.

I'm not a coffee drinker, but I know people like free coffee, and the presentations were amazing. Tina also always had a videographer present to capture the talks, and she posted every event online, building up an archive of past gatherings. The popularity of *CreativeMornings* in New York soared—it got to the point where Tina would wait to open tickets the Monday before the Friday event, and the free tickets would vanish in a matter of hours. Later, they would disappear in minutes. Word spread to people in other cities and folks started getting very interested in CreativeMornings, so Tina had the idea to expand the concept to other cities. In the spring of 2011, she put out a call for volunteer event organizers in a number of key cities, including Boston. I saw the opportunity immediately. Here was an existing brand and event format that we could take on and have an audience and platform from day one.

I didn't hesitate. In fact, I didn't even consult the team or our board. The minute I saw the call for a Boston organizer, I applied. In many ways, the Design Museum and I were the perfect applicants for *CreativeMornings* in Boston. Just as we would benefit from an existing brand and platform, they would as well—from day one, the Design Museum Boston audience would be introduced to *CreativeMornings*. Once again, everyone won. Tina and her team chose me to be the Boston organizer, and right away, the Design Museum volunteer team and I got to work planning our first CreativeMornings Boston event.

In true Design Museum fashion, our *CreativeMornings* events would pop up in various places around the city. For the first, I partnered with a small co-working space right near Boston's South Station called WorkBar. They hosted and provided free coffee and danishes. I asked a long-time supporter of mine, and an amazing design thinker, Richard Watson of Essential

Design, to be our first presenter and share a bit of his design philosophy and process. The first event was a big success, drawing in eighty people, and the series was successful as well —folks loved that they could count on a fun, monthly event where they could network and find community as well as learn from a local design thought leader. Both brands, Design Museum and *CreativeMornings*, experienced an immediate halo effect that grew both audiences in town. Everybody won.

———————

With each opportunity, we were building our credibility with partners and growing our audience. But we needed a way to accelerate turning Design Museum Boston into a revenue-generating business. We had a few one-off, five-figure sponsors here and there, but no annually recurring revenue or predictable revenue of any kind—nothing with which to build a foundation for the organization. We were constantly looking for ways to boost our profile, recruit mentors and advisors, and grow the business in any way we could.

Around the same time we started Design Museum Boston, a number of other really interesting organizations started up as well. One that played a big part in our growth was MassChallenge. Founded in 2009, MassChallenge is a nonprofit startup accelerator. Startups apply to participate, and the ones chosen receive office space, mentorship from top industry experts, and a chance to pitch for funding. When I learned about MassChallenge in 2010, I immediately thought Design Museum Boston was perfect for the program and that we would benefit a lot from the intentional acceleration they were offering. But looking at the companies they were choosing for the program, I felt like the Design Museum wasn't ready. We were just getting started, and while MassChallenge was taking in very early-stage companies, most were high-growth/high-potential for-profit companies—we were a tiny nonprofit with no revenue model.

I wanted to apply, but I thought the effort would be wasted since we weren't yet compelling enough to be chosen by the judges—plus, their application process was very opaque. I wouldn't know how to optimize our chances unless I could get a peek at the application and process. The only way to understand that was to apply, which gave me an idea.

When applications opened in early 2011, I made up a fake company and applied for MassChallenge's startup accelerator. MassChallenge was that open—you could apply with the kernel of an idea, but you needed to make it through multiple rounds of consideration. I used an idea for a business I came up with for one of my business courses at Babson. I called it Massive, and it was sort of an event and A/V equipment on-demand service. If you were having an event, you could go online, choose the equipment you needed through a graphical configurator tool, choose a date, and a technician would bring the equipment, set it up, and then return to take it down. Think digital projectors, microphones, and PA systems. It was a neat little business idea, but not a real one.

I used Massive to go through the application process, and I took notes the whole time so I could optimize Design Museum's application the next time around. First, there was the written application, which would be judged by a panel of experts—I copied down all the questions for next year. Then there was a round of public voting—basically, an online popularity contest to get as many votes as possible. That was very interesting for next year, if we could galvanize our growing community I figured we could be one of the top vote-getters. If you made it through the written application and the public voting phase—which I didn't with Massive, thankfully—you then pitched to a group of judges via Skype. That meant we needed a very compelling pitch deck and presentation.

I went through all the motions using my fake company to apply for the 2011 cohort of MassChallenge, but of course, never made it to the second round of judging. That wasn't the point. I learned a ton about how to apply with Design Museum Boston. So when the applications opened for the 2012 cohort, we were very ready. Our written application was tight, and after a successful 2011, we had a lot in there to be proud of and impress the judges with. Prior to the public voting, we primed our online community that this was coming and what we needed them to do: vote and tell their friends and family to vote. Our community never disappointed us.

By the time MassChallenge's public voting period closed, Design Museum Boston was the top vote-getter. We made it to the second round of judging, and again, we were ready. Our slide deck and pitch were solid. Derek and I presented to a panel of judges, and it was clear they were all very intrigued by our unique approach that had the potential to disrupt the museum field. While we weren't a high-growth tech company, we did have a lot of potential for growth with the right mentorship and resources.

On May 29, 2012, MassChallenge announced their 2012 cohort, and Design Museum Boston was in. In late June, we moved into their class-A office space in a new tower in Boston's Seaport—now we had an office. We went through a series of matchmaking events and were paired with three amazing mentors, Ed Loessi, Ed Ross, and Sharon Kan. We took part in training sessions to learn how to better grow our business and continued to build our network thanks to the visibility we received as a MassChallenge startup. We wanted to get the most out of our experience there and focused our time and sessions with our mentors on how to monetize the museum and become a sustainable business. We also popped up an exhibition in the MassChallenge lobby and held a series of events on how design can help startups. It was another win for everyone.

———————

Our friend Jason Schupbach, the person who made all those connections for us when he was the Creative Economy Director in Massachusetts, eventually moved on to a new job at the National Endowment for the Arts focused on creative placemaking. If you think about the public places you love, what makes them special? Creative placemaking means using art and design to define, establish, and retain a place for a community. It could be something as simple as designing a public park with elements of art that reflect the local community or working with a city to create and brand a public square that holds public theater performances every week. Creative placemaking was a burgeoning field aimed at being intentional about turning spaces into places that people love. Early in Jason's tenure, the NEA launched a new grant program for creative placemaking called *Our Town*. The idea was to fund partnerships between nonprofits using art and design in public places and city governments to support new placemaking efforts around the country.

When I first learned about *Our Town* and read the guidelines, I couldn't help thinking that Jason had designed this program with Design Museum Boston in mind. They were looking for organizations that operated in partnership with the community, engaging in public programming in cities and towns, and were adept at experimenting with new models for turning spaces into dynamic public environments. That was the Design Museum. We built an incredible community in Boston. We were popping up in places around the city. We added a new level of activity and dynamism that inspired people everywhere we went. We were creating *place*. Once again, I saw an opportunity here to take the museum to the next level, and this opportunity had dollar signs attached to it.

There were two hurdles to overcome. One was Design Museum Boston was not yet a registered 501(c)3 nonprofit organization, which meant we could not accept tax-deductible donations or apply for public grants. But the second hurdle could help me overcome that: the NEA wanted to fund partnerships between organizations. A partnership with the local government was required; the highest-ranking public official in the city or town where the project would take place had to provide a signed letter of support. In the case of Boston, I needed a signed letter from the legendary Mayor Thomas Menino.

In 2009 and 2010, the Menino administration was looking for ways to kickstart urban development in the latter half of the Great Recession. Boston's Seaport was a concrete and asphalt wasteland—for the most part—that they saw as the next area of urban development. Once you crossed the Fort Point Channel bridges from the Downtown Financial District, you were met with old brick buildings that housed a vibrant arts community—rent was cheap, and the buildings were no frills. There were empty lots as far as the eye could see (until you went farther east to the Marine Industrial Park where fish was still being processed, Harpoon Brewery made their beer, and various other warehousing and light industrial companies utilized the active port).

Mayor Menino's vision was to turn the Seaport into Boston's next new neighborhood, a place that supported startup companies, creative pursuits, and big businesses. They dubbed the Seaport the "Innovation District," and it became somewhat of a startup within the city of Boston. They created a brand for it, a website, and a community. Mayor Menino gave speeches about it, and they worked with corporations and real estate developers to set a vision for what this new neighborhood could be. It was exciting! Most of Boston was developed and literally set in stone—this was an opportunity to create something new and different. It wasn't all roses, though. There was conflict—and in conflict, there can be opportunity.

The City of Boston was engaged in a placemaking effort, whether they called it that or not. The trouble was that the Seaport was already a place, home to the largest artist community in New England: the Fort Point Artist Community, or FPAC for short. FPAC rightly claimed that the Seaport was already a community filled with vibrant art and artists that needed the city's support to remain sustainable. The city's vision of big companies making their headquarters in the Seaport contoured visions of rising rents, expensive restaurants, and, ultimately, the loss of the artist community. I saw an opportunity in that standoff between business and creative interests. What else sits at the intersection between business and creativity? Design. I believed Design Museum Boston could play a role in preserving the creative community in Fort Point while also supporting the urban and business development Mayor Menino envisioned for the Innovation District. Through public programming like events, exhibitions, workshops, youth programs, and more, the museum could be a central organization in making the Seaport a vibrant place where, in Menino's words, people could live, work, and play.

The Innovation District initiative was run through the City's business development office, run by our friends Randi Lathrop and Kristin Phelan, whom we worked with to bring our *Creative Capital* exhibition to Boston City Hall. So with *Creative Capital* still gracing the walls and floors of their office, I met with Randi and Kristin in early 2011 to share the *Our Town* opportunity and my vision for how Design Museum Boston could play a role in the Innovation District. They loved it and would work with the mayor's office to get the required letter of support.

It turned out that having *Creative Capital* at Boston City Hall was one of the most strategic things we could have done in our early days. Leaders, power brokers, and decision-makers from across the city visited Boston Redevelopment Authority's offices regularly. And while they walked the hallways of the BRA's office, they were learning about Design Museum Boston. That made everything easier, including getting the mayor's signature on a letter in support of our *Our Town* grant proposal. I still needed a nonprofit partner, an organization that would not only write and receive the grant but would add credibility to our application. Design Museum Boston was still a tiny organization with about $5,000 in our bank account. I was worried we wouldn't be taken seriously by the NEA, even with the partnership with the City of Boston.

From my meetings with President Kay Sloan, I knew that Massachusetts College of Art and Design wanted to become more involved in the city. As a publicly funded art school, with its own tower in Boston, it was a bit siloed from the community around it. Kay wanted to connect the school and the students to the city in ways that made their MassArt experience unique. MassArt was also still incubating DIGMA, the Design Industry Group of Massachusetts, as a way to bolster creative businesses across the commonwealth. There was my partnership. I saw it so clearly.

I met with MassArt's director of continuing education, Anne Marie Stein, who was also the liaison between MassArt and DIGMA. I shared my ideas for how Design Museum Boston, the City of Boston, MassArt, and DIGMA could partner, apply for *Our Town* grant funds, and make a huge impact on the Seaport. Anne Marie loved it—here was a chance to align MassArt with a major city initiative. It was a way to connect DIGMA with the businesses they wanted to infuse with design, the city would benefit from vibrant public programming, and Design Museum Boston could show our unique capabilities for creative placemaking and grow in the process. Win, win, win, win—everyone wins.

The crucial element here was that MassArt would actually be applying for the grant. As a nonprofit organization, they were eligible, and they had an entire development department filled with experienced grant writers. The process taught me so much about grant writing. I explained the vision in broad terms: we would apply for funding in support of placemaking initiatives in Boston's burgeoning Innovation District to ensure livability for all residents, sustain a vibrant creative community, and create jobs by supporting small businesses and attracting large employers to the neighborhood. The vision aligned with Mayor Menino's desires for the neighborhood and fit perfectly within the NEA's guidelines for *Our Town*. We hit submit on the grant in early 2011 and waited.

In July 2011, when the first round of *Our Town* grants was announced, we were awarded a $50,000 grant for our project in the Innovation District. Success! The resulting funds, plus the funds we raised to match the NEA grant, allowed our partnership to hire me as a contractor to carry out the project. This was a win for all, but a major win for the new-on-the-scene Design Museum. For the first time, there would be someone being paid to work on the museum.

———

Each opportunity built on the last. I began the Innovation District project by immersing myself in the Fort Point and Seaport communities. Announcing that a partnership between the City of Boston, Massachusetts College of Art and Design, the Design Industry Group of Massachusetts, and Design Museum Boston received a major grant to activate the Innovation District through creative placemaking and public programming got a lot of attention. And in our case, there was a major curiosity factor. Folks saw the announcement and articles in the local paper, and I know they thought to themselves, "Wait, Boston has a design museum?"

I started connecting with anyone and everyone who would take a meeting with me. I studied and mapped the existing community on the ground. I needed to meet with community leaders, the folks who led the artist community, city and state officials, business leaders, and leaders of the growing startup community. Through our existing community, connections from my partners on the grant, and good old-fashioned cold outreach, I started meeting with the key people in the neighborhood. It began as one-on-one meetings where community leaders were trying to understand what the museum even was, and, honestly, whether they could trust us or not. Trust building was the name of the game, and my intentions were pure. I wanted to use design to make this area more livable and bring the various communities together for a common purpose.

Meetings led to more meetings as folks were inspired by Design Museum's vision for creative public programming in the district. People would say, "This sounds great. You really need to meet with my contact over at..." and that would lead to the next organization I would meet with. That's what I did for the first few months of the project. I made my ecosystem map of the existing communities and methodically worked to connect with as many people as possible. The one-on-one meetings eventually shifted to meetings with groups of people so we could share the message and recruit folks to our vision at scale. We planned the first in a series of town hall meetings that would be open to the public. These would be listening sessions where we would outline the original vision for the grant, but more importantly, we'd learn what folks who lived and worked in the district wanted and needed from this burgeoning neighborhood. We needed a location for the first town hall, and, fortunately, I was connected to the kind folks at Grand Circle Gallery, Mark Schianca and Shirley Barkai.

Mark ran a small gallery on the ground level of the Grand Circle Travel building in Fort Point. Grant Circle was primarily a cruise and travel agency that created unique group trips for seniors to see the world. Over the course of a lifetime, the founding owners traveled the world and amassed an amazing curation of unique cultural artifacts and a huge collection of travel posters. These were on display across various themed exhibitions created by Mark and Shirley in the street-level gallery. When I met with Mark the first time, he was so intrigued by our unique concept, having come from the museum industry. I let him know we needed an event space to host roughly seventy people for our first town hall, and he was happy to oblige and offer up the gallery space.

The town hall was great, but we wanted to do more together. Mark was looking for ways to activate the gallery and, in particular, showcase the design of the hundreds of travel posters in Grand Circle's collection. The posters were visual artifacts of fantastic artistry and design, depicting exotic locales through color, form, illustration, and craft. Mark was sitting on one of the biggest graphic design collections I had ever come in contact with. He openly wondered and then proposed a partnership between Design Museum Boston and Grand Circle Gallery. He wanted to know how we could collaborate and produce some sort of travel-themed exhibition.

Fresh off our *Creative Capital* and *Retail* exhibitions, the Design Museum team was very interested in continuing to show the public how the world around us is designed. So we proposed to Mark an idea: an exhibition that would uncover the design of the travel experience. We would show how everything from airports, planes, and ships to flight attendant uniforms, luggage, wayfinding, and signage was designed and who designed it—all against the backdrop of Grand Circle's collection of vintage travel posters. Mark and Shirley loved it, and Grand Circle Travel agreed to sponsor the exhibition development.

We got to work curating the content for the show. Our friends at Samsonite let us raid their archive, and we uncovered design work from the 1940s and 50s for the first roller suitcase. We connected with designers at Teague, a design firm founded by Walter Dorwin Teague, who helped design the first commercial airplanes in the early 20th century. We poured through Grand Circle's travel poster collection for

Derek Cascio leaning on a display case at Getting There at Logan Airport, 2012. Photo: John Gillooly

examples of beautiful graphic design. The result was an exhibition called *Getting There: Design for Travel in the Modern Age.*

In late April 2012, my wife Nicole and I moved to Fort Point in Boston's Seaport District, securing a coveted live/work studio so Nicole could truly transition to being a full-time ceramic artist. Our loft was just down the street from Grand Circle Gallery, so before we moved in, Derek and I converted it into a makeshift exhibition fabrication facility. For three solid days, Derek, my parents (Sam and Wendy), and I fabricated the exhibition from scratch in that apartment. Then on May 10, 2012, we opened *Getting There* at Grand Circle Gallery with a reception for our members and donors. The show was a lot of fun and helped transport people through time and into the design studios of creators around the world working on the travel experience.

In true Design Museum form, once again, each opportunity built on the last. Derek had a brilliant idea to bring this exhibition to Logan Airport. What better venue for an exhibition on travel and design than Boston's travel hub? He scored a partnership with Massport's real estate team, along with another big sponsorship from Samsonite, to make it happen. We took the opportunity to improve and redesign *Getting There* from the ground up—if it was going to survive being in Terminal E with hundreds of thousands of people, we needed to make it more robust.

On November 15, 2012, we opened *Getting There* in Logan Airport's International Terminal E with another big reception, once again proving ourselves able to develop intriguing, well-curated exhibitions and pop them up in places people already go.

———————

For those counting, those were seven opportunities that accelerated the Design Museum into the business it is today. What are the opportunities you're going to find, create, or stumble into? Your job as a founder is finding or making opportunities for your business. Period. The key for us was being open to partnerships and collaborations that could more quickly get us to our audience. Look for opportunities like accelerator programs that make you stretch a bit and kick you into a new level of operations and revenue.

Each one of the opportunities I mentioned—taking on *CreativeMornings Boston,* building a partnership to pursue a National Endowment for the Arts Grant, launching an exhibition at Logan Airport—was a bit outside our comfort zone, and we had to grow and partner to make them happen. We didn't create everything or own everything in these opportunities. We may have catalyzed things, but it was all about sharing ownership and sharing successes. The key is to create win-wins that benefit you and your partner and build relationships that will last the life of your business and beyond.

If we're thinking about our cupcake shop and mail-order business, perhaps we build a relationship with some of the local places where people celebrate birthdays. Say your birthday is at the local brewery. We'll give you a discount on cupcakes and deliver them to the party fresh. Or maybe we help organize a local food festival—customers will learn about all the good stuff made right in their community, including our shop. For *Art Scouts,* I've already mentioned partnerships with children's museums and community centers, places where people gather and where parents want their kids to have an educational experience. Like the Design Museum, we could also partner with other nonprofits to seek sponsorship or grant funding for our programs.

Our exhibition design course at Wentworth Institute of Technology—the one that spawned the *Retail* exhibition at Prudential Center Mall—was so well received by the students, the college, and the public, that the administration at Wentworth asked me and Derek to do it again. This time, I'm proud to say the students learned from our partnership-building, win-win savviness. In 2012, the International Industrial Designers Society of America conference was coming to Boston. Design Museum Boston was making so many waves that the chairman of the society, Austen Angell, invited Derek and me to speak as keynote presenters. The students had an idea.

Every year, IDSA held its Industrial Design Excellence Awards celebrating the best industrial design coming from the industry. And every year, there was a pretty lackluster exhibition of the finalists at the national conference. The students wanted to truly celebrate and elevate the winners of IDEA with a Design Museum Boston exhibition—it was brilliant. Again, the students did it all—Derek and I were there as professors, coaching and supporting—but the students curated the work from the IDEA winners, everything from a forklift to medical equipment, consumer products, and more. They collected artifacts and stories from the design teams. They raised funds through a Kickstarter crowdfunding campaign and secured sponsors.

On August 15, 2012, the students opened *Life Impacted: International Design Excellence Exhibition* at the Westin Waterfront Hotel as part of the IDSA's International Conference. With the exhibition on view and Derek and me speaking about the museum to over a thousand people at the conference, it felt like a full-circle moment. In 2008, we were running the Boston IDSA chapter as two young designers trying to build community. Four years later, we were museum founders sharing our vision and our progress at an international conference.

CHAPTER 10

Monetize or Dawdle

Let's make some money.

"If a company isn't making money, you don't have a successful venture; you have a hobby."

—Jeff Sutherland, creator of scrum project management

In early 2012, the Design Museum was still very much a volunteer-run side hustle for me and the team. We knew we were building something special and important, but it just wasn't our sole focus because, frankly, Design Museum Boston didn't pay our bills. Thanks to the National Endowment for the Arts *Our Town* grant, I did have a nice contract with MassArt to begin our creative placemaking work in the Innovation District, so I was getting closer to the museum as a paying job. But building the business and securing revenue just wasn't our focus in the first few years.

We knew starting a nonprofit was risky, so we kept our jobs and focused on building a community. As important as that was, the community wasn't going to generate revenue for us unless we did something about it. Being accepted into MassChallenge, the eight-month startup accelerator, changed that math for us. For the Design Museum, acceleration meant monetization and building a sustainable revenue model. While we didn't receive any funding from the accelerator, we decided to use our time at MassChallenge to figure out how to turn this idea for a one-of-a-kind nomadic museum into something sustainable long-term.

Thankfully, we didn't have to do this alone—once again, our community did not disappoint. In September 2011, I received an email from Scott Reilly. Scott would end up being one of the most important people in our startup journey and a key mentor to me in launching and growing the museum. Scott had recently moved back to Boston from Atlanta to be near his aging parents. He was an expert in brick-and-mortar design retail, and he was one of the first people to market and sell contemporary design on the Internet to make it more accessible to people everywhere. He was a design curator with deep knowledge across various movements and countries. He served on the boards of multiple arts and design organizations in the Atlanta area and, in his words, was focused on "special events, marketing, earned revenue opportunities, web content, membership drives, and fundraising." Sometimes you get lucky. But you make your own luck; our online presence is what piqued Scott's interest. He was just the type of volunteer and advisor we needed at the time.

We set up lunch with Scott, who ended up volunteering and eventually joined our Board of Directors. Scott is one-of-a-kind—always sporting some variation of a dark turtleneck and jeans, always looking the part of a design curator, but never with an ego. He's one of the warmest, funniest people

I've ever met and yet, somehow, also introverted and extremely thoughtful. We became fast friends, and I'm grateful for his mentorship. He saw immediately what Derek and I knew deep down but wouldn't admit: we were so focused on creating exhibitions and events, connecting with our community, and maintaining our beautiful web presence that we weren't paying enough attention to raising money and making the Design Museum a viable business.

We had some online donations coming in, and we might occasionally fall into a corporate sponsorship as we did with Samsonite. But there was no focused effort to make money. We had a hobby on our hands, but I desperately wanted to turn it into a business that had staying power. One of the main reasons I wanted to start the Design Museum was I loved bringing people together for events, exhibitions, education programs, networking, parties, and more—and I was good at it. But Scott gave me the most important advice anyone ever gave me as a young entrepreneur building a business. He said, "Sam, if you want the Design Museum to succeed, you are no longer the programming or exhibition creator, or the event producer, or the community manager. You need to be the lead fundraiser. Let other people create and manage the museum's programs and outreach. There is no one on the team that's going to be better at generating revenue for this vision than you. And you need to start now."

Scott's advice came at such a key time. In 2012, we were all feeling burned out. Working a full-time job and building a business on the side will do that. I came to an important realization with Scott's help that may seem obvious, but it wasn't clear to me at that time until our team started showing real signs of fatigue: it was my job as the founder to figure out how we were going to make money because if we didn't, the museum maybe wouldn't die immediately, but we would sort of dawdle around for a few years, plateau, get tired, and then, eventually, die. At the pace required to launch our startup, with all the other parts of life and work, there was no way the team could sustain this half-in, half-out approach long-term.

———

My goal was to create a business that was not only profitable but had a sustainable business model that would be adaptable to changing conditions in the market. Contrast that with the Design Museum in 2012 when we were giving everything away to our audience for free. Exhibitions were free and open to the public, events were free, access to our community was free—it was all free, free, free. And that was okay for a time. Initially, we didn't have to worry about capturing value and making money because this was still our side project. We also wanted to be as accessible as possible. Giving everything away for free made us happy and fit our values.

Scott's advice here was simple: emulate the business model of every other museum in the world. Why reinvent the wheel? Museums have existed for thousands of years. Museums charge admission, have membership programs, charge for rentals, cultivate philanthropic donors, and those are just a few of the possible revenue mechanisms. I initially—and wrongly —pushed back on Scott's advice. I thought we were different —in some ways, we were. We were disrupting the museum world and making something new and better. So I thought our business model had to be equally different and innovative to match this new approach of a museum without a building. Luckily, I had great (and patient) advisors like Scott, the other members of our board, and our mentors at MassChallenge to help me see that yes, we were totally disrupting how a museum delivers value, but that didn't mean we had to start from scratch on how a museum captures value.

We started by thinking through how we would fund the development of our key programs: exhibitions and events. Think of these as our product lines or service offerings. Each had real costs associated with them. Exhibitions are, by their nature, very capital-intensive projects. Not only do you need to conceive the idea, but then there's the curation, relationship building with content providers, developing and interpreting the content, artifact and asset gathering—it's a lot of thought and outreach work. It's a lot of time for an expert or experts to spend doing something, and, of course, time is money. Then there are the hard costs of the physical materials like displays, printed panels, vinyl wall wraps, security measures, audio/ visual equipment, and more.

Exhibitions are expensive in a way that all the costs are upfront. They're capital-intensive—you typically don't get a return on your capital investment until after you've spent everything it takes to create the thing. Most museums charge an admission fee to see exhibitions, and some even charge an additional fee or require an additional ticket purchase for special exhibitions. Since we didn't have our own building, we couldn't control entry; therefore, we couldn't charge for exhibition entry. We also really didn't want to charge for our exhibitions—we held onto the core value that we wanted our exhibitions to be as accessible as possible. So we made a fundamental decision that all our exhibitions would be free and open to the public. That didn't help our revenue problem at all. We determined the museum needed a program to develop seed funding to invest in our exhibitions and some way we could build recurring revenue from our amazing community of supporters. Scott Reilly made it his mission to push us forward.

Derek and I secured corporate sponsors for various programs, even going back to our days running the Boston chapter of the Industrial Designers Society of America. A good example was our *Getting There* exhibition at Logan Airport—we proudly shared with Scott that we successfully pitched Massport to sponsor the exhibition for $7,000. When we shared that number, Scott almost fell off his chair, "That's all?!" he exclaimed. We shared that $7,000 covered our costs for fabricating and printing the exhibition, so we were good. But we were wrong. We were not good.

Scott opened our eyes to a key fact: we needed to fund the full scope of the program, which included our time curating, developing, and designing the exhibitions. Funding our time had not been a priority because we all had jobs. But if we wanted to make the Design Museum our job, in Scott's words, we needed to "over-fund" each program to take our time into account and make profits we could re-invest into the business. Scott's advice was not to just find one sponsor that covers the hard costs and then stop. Instead, we needed to find as many sponsors as possible.

He pushed us to treat our sponsor-finding efforts as a program itself, worthy of program management, time, and focus. That clicked for me. If getting sponsor revenue was a project—and I love projects—then that was something I could apply my creativity and efforts to and, in doing so, pre-fund everything we wanted to do with exhibitions and more. With Scott's guidance, we started thinking about everything we were doing as a program that could be funded through sponsorship.

In a for-profit company, this might be more like pitching for marketing partnerships or investment. For each program, be it an exhibition or event series, we created a one-sheet, front and back—or sometimes a four-sheet, bi-folded booklet—that described the program, primary audience, ways our sponsors could be involved and directly engage with us and our audience, and the most important piece, sponsorship levels and benefits of sponsoring at each level.

We created a sales pipeline of organizations to meet with that included pretty much every design-oriented company in the Greater Boston area. We cold-called or found introductions through board members or others in our community—and we could usually get a meeting. At the meeting, we introduced ourselves and the museum, but most importantly, we asked questions about the company and how they envisioned interacting with the design community. While they were talking and we were listening, we were also forming alignments between their vision and our programs, and we could almost always find some alignment. This required us to be authentically listening while simultaneously crafting our pitch in the back of our minds—and Derek and I had to be in sync, without being able to actually talk to each other in the meeting.

We got so good at reading each other and building off what the other person was saying. It was like improv—and because there were two of us, usually pitching one or two people, there was this social power to it. If there were three of us in a room, Derek and I were in agreement, so the third person (the one we were selling) had just a bit of social pressure to also agree with us. Our passion for this work certainly didn't hurt either. If Derek and I could score the meeting, there was a very good chance we were walking out of that meeting with a verbal commitment.

So let's say the person we were meeting with wanted to host a cool design event in their space—we would pull out the *UNITE* sponsor booklet and start talking about how great *UNITE* events are and how awesome it would be to have an event in their space. We could already see the event in our heads, so we'd use that imagery to get the sponsor excited as well. The costs of sponsoring an event were right there in the packet, mixed in with the photos, so while we were talking about the event and pointing to the photos, the prospective sponsor was seeing the costs and doing the math in their head.

At the end of each meeting—and this is the crucial step—we'd gauge their interest and then ask if we could follow up with a written proposal to support the planning and production of a *UNITE* event in their space. Within twenty-four hours, I'd write a summary of our meeting on Design Museum letterhead, along with the costs (or a few options if there were different levels we talked about in the meeting), and we sent it to the contact, asking if we could count them in. Don't ever forget to make the ask. Sometimes folks said no, but many times they said yes—then I'd follow up with basically the same document, except this time, I called it a sponsorship agreement. Once they signed and returned the agreement, I sent them an invoice for the amount. Cue the cash register sound. Money was on its way.

———

We focused on sponsorships first because of the quicker cash cycle, i.e., the time between closing the deal and getting the actual money in your business account. But grants were next on our list. Grants are similar to sponsorships but with a longer cash cycle. With sponsors, we would typically get cash within thirty to sixty days. That's good for cash flow because you need to spend some of that money on your program (or product) expenses as soon as possible. Grants have a long cash cycle—sometimes very long. Before you see one dime of grant money, you need to research grants and decide if you're eligible and meet the funding criteria. Sometimes you need to meet with grant officers and sell them before you can even apply. You need to write the grant, create visual samples, apply, and then wait. Sometimes, you wait months and months, and then you get rejected. That's rough since you've put in so much effort in the sales process, and now you're done—although, if you're smart, you can use those same grant materials for other grants.

Let's say you actually get chosen for the grant funding—in rare cases, you'll get a check right away. Most times you either need to wait another month or three for the money, or many grants will require you to spend the money first, and then they will reimburse you. So you spend money you don't have, invoice the granting organization, and wait thirty to sixty days for the money. That is a long cash cycle that can be painful for your business.

I started researching grants and foundations and applying. I learned so much about grant writing by being part of the National Endowment for the Arts *Our Town* application with MassArt and the City of Boston, and I applied my learnings to future grants. I took a lot of swings, and I got a lot of rejections at first, but there is a cool feedback loop with grants. Some granting organizations, when they reject you, are open to a follow-up call to give you feedback. With that feedback loop, I honed my approach. I learned to love writing grants—

it was a chance to be creative, set a vision, and persuade people through my writing.

————

Over time, it started to work. We eventually started securing grant funding (large and small) for our programs. We were putting in the effort, and our revenue from sponsors and grants blossomed through 2012. Fundraising wasn't this side thing we were doing to cover our hard costs. It was turning into a core competency and function for our company. There was only one problem with this revenue model. It was always necessary to have a new program to sell to sponsors. When we didn't have a new program to sell, we had no way to make money or grow. Consequently, this sometimes led us to create programs just so we'd have something to sell—which put us in a very rough position a few times since our team only had the capacity to do so many things at once.

When you get sponsorship money or grant money for a project, you need to actually do the project, and in doing so, you end up spending a good portion of that money to actually produce the program. We were running our operations on the meager profits of our programs—we had very little money left over after producing everything to reinvest in the organization. We needed an ongoing revenue source that wasn't tied so tightly to the programs we produced because, in reality, we were a small team who could handle producing perhaps an event or two each month, and a major exhibition every one to two years.

To gain revenue not specifically tied to launching new, expensive programs, Scott Reilly had the solution: offer a membership program. Most museums have them. Members

usually pay monthly or annually at various levels for an array
of benefits. This is the coveted annual recurring revenue
(ARR) that so many startups seek—and you should too, no
matter what your business is. Together, we started outlining
what a membership program could look like. What would
members of the Design Museum get if they could already go
to our exhibitions and events for free? One conversation went
something like this.

Scott: "How are event ticket sales going?"

Me: "We don't charge for tickets."

Scott: "Why the heck not?!"

So part of our new membership strategy was to start
charging non-members (or not-yet-members) for event tickets,
and members would continue to attend for free. With events,
we actually did control entry through our website and
registration tables onsite. In creating membership as a revenue
stream, we also unlocked ticket sales as an additional stream.

We designed the entire member experience, every
touchpoint. We put a value on exclusive access and close
connection to both the museum and us as founders. Members
would receive a membership card with their name and
member number, and it would grant them special access to
exhibition opening receptions, tours of exhibitions from Derek
and me, swag like t-shirts and tote bags, and even access to
special events.

Derek designed the perfect membership card for us. It was
a lenticular print, sort of like those old-school holographic
baseball cards where there were two images printed on the
same surface, and depending on how you rotated the card,
you'd see one or the other. The baseball cards usually showed
the batter swinging the bat. In our case, as you slightly turned
the card from side to side, it looked like the "D" logo was

Lenticular Design Museum Boston membership card.

exploding and coming back together. It was so neat. We planned a big special event to introduce membership to our community for September 20, 2012. There was only one problem: we had no way of actually accepting credit card payments. This is a non-issue these days with plenty of online services, cloud payment portals, and cart options—think Stripe or Shopify. But Stripe didn't exist in 2012. I took this on, even though I had no payment processing or coding experience, but I was determined to figure it out.

I am not a programmer or a coder or a hacker, but the night before the membership launch, I finally found a way to link Salesforce with Authorize.net, an early version of services like Stripe where you could accept credit card payments online. I found a third-party plugin that would link them and allow for recurring transactions—but I had to code a lot of the integration myself. I still don't know how I did that, except that there was a lot of trial and error and online tutorials that night. I finally went to sleep at 7 am the next day, but I got it done.

At the membership launch party, we announced our big offer—this was Scott's brilliant idea—if you became a member at the membership launch party or anytime between then and December 31, 2012, we would designate you a Founding Member, and as long as you kept renewing every year, you'd keep that status forever. This cost us nothing. It was a little extra ink on the back of the membership cards. That was it, but people loved it. I love this kind of stuff, too. They were proud to be with us at the beginning and wanted to be recognized for their early support.

That night, we sold so many memberships, it was as if people were just waiting for a real way to support us, to solidify their place in our community. Folks became official, card-carrying members of the Design Museum Boston community. And over the next three months, founding member numbers continued to climb. Scott was right. This was it: annual recurring revenue from our community of supporters that wasn't tied to any specific program or project. People wanted to be part of this museum and support our work—and the member benefits were nice as well! From September to December 2012, membership revenue soared.

———

Meeting Scott probably was a bit of luck, but listening to his guidance was a choice. Through his mentorship and guidance, he turned Derek and me into money-raising machines. The exciting part of designing your business is you can borrow what works best, innovate every bit of the model, prototype things, and try it out. Did it make money? Keep it.

Did it confuse your customers? Drop it. I regularly told Derek, as we were trying to figure out our business model, that I felt like we were the raptors in the cage in Jurassic Park—constantly hitting and testing the fence, looking for a weak point where we could break through and wreak havoc. Perhaps I had that visual in mind when working with Proportion Design on the cover of this book.

For all the amazing advice I received from Scott and others on revenue generation, I got a lot of bad advice as well. Someone once told me to pick a revenue stream and stick to it. If I did that, the museum would have failed years ago. One model wasn't going to be enough, and even if it was enough, how would you know which model to double down on so early in your business-building adventure? Creative ventures sometimes require multi-faceted business models. I like to call it the business model quilt, the patchwork of models that make your unique, creative startup work and make money. There are a ton of established business models to explore and mix and match, to try and refine and put your own spin on. There's direct sales, consulting, peer-to-peer, freemium, multi-sided platform, razor and blade, membership, direct-to-consumer, and the list goes on.

Your job is to apply a model or models so your business turns a profit. You can experiment, try things, create little prototypes and tests, and see what's successful. If your venture is community-based—and I believe every business is community-based—I recommend thinking hard about membership. Membership is a great way to monetize your community, generate annual recurring revenue, and build strong affiliations with people and even other businesses.

For our cupcake business, perhaps there is a *Cupcake of the Month* membership where we ship a new set of cupcakes each month to folks who pay for a membership or maybe they can utilize their membership at the shop for free samples. For *Art Scouts*, perhaps you need to be a member to even participate in our art classes. Or there could be a project box that we ship to members monthly with instructions for them to do at home on their own or as part of live-streamed video classes.

I'll give you the same advice Scott Reilly gave me. You may have started your business because you love the product or the service or the offering, but no matter what, you are the best and primary salesperson for your business. As the founder, you have the story, the passion, and the commitment that no one else outside your founding team has. It's up to you to figure out a business model or patchwork quilt of models that generates enough revenue for sustainability, and then sell, sell, sell. And by sell, I mean constantly turn the crank of your business model to ensure cash flow, the lifeblood of your business.

A smart strategy is determining how you can secure some seed funding. I like to think about this funding as money in before you take on major expenses—it's money to plant the seed and watch it grow. There are a few ways to do this. Derek and I bootstrapped our seed funding, which is a fancy way of saying we used our own money, kept expenses down, and pulled ourselves up from nothing but our… bootstraps.

Another popular approach is pre-selling or using pre-orders. This is a great idea for highly anticipated goods or services that may already have a strong community around them. You often see authors allowing their readers to pre-order their books months before the actual release. Or you may pre-order a video game that you've heard great things about so you can play it on the first day it comes out. Crowdfunding is a similar approach. You can use a platform like Kickstarter or Indiegogo to market your offering, build a community, and ask folks to back the work before it's complete—the resulting funds help you bring your offering over the finish line and to the market.

Startup accelerators or incubators are other great places for seed funding. We didn't receive funding from MassChallenge, but other startups did. The nice thing about MassChallenge is they take no equity—or ownership stake—in the startups they support. Other startup incubators ask for an equity stake in your company in exchange for seed funding, mentorship, and office space.

Like Design Museum, you can also pursue grants as a nonprofit or find grants for small business development as a for-profit company. Check out the Small Business Administration's (SBA) programs, as well as offerings from companies like FedEx, which offers a competitive small business grant program. There are small business loans backed by the SBA, as well as loans from your local bank.

There are also credit cards. Not my top recommendation, but I know plenty of founders who used credit cards to buy their startup equipment, finance their first bit of inventory, and more—then they worked their tails off to generate the surplus revenue to pay off the high-interest debt. We used credit cards quite a bit to smooth out major swings in our cash flow over the years.

Through 2012, and especially September through December with our Founding membership launch and campaign, roughly 40% of our revenue was coming from project-based funding like corporate sponsors and ticket sales; another 50% came from our membership program; and the last 10% was from grants. These percentages would dramatically change over the years as we shifted our focus to meet our needs and align with the market. But because of that new revenue, our runway—the time between now and when your cash runs out—was looking better than ever, and we did two important things.

Our time at the MassChallenge accelerator came to an end, which meant we were going to lose our free office space—so we leased our first official office space at 12 Channel Street in Boston's Marine Industrial Park. It was a great space that allowed us to have an office, conference room, and a sizable fabrication shop. Plus it had freight elevators and a large loading dock.

Even more importantly, Derek and I hired each other as the first full-time employees of the Design Museum. We like to say we both aced the interview process. Both of us had the title Director, and we agreed to pay each other the same salary, $30,000/year. A low salary to be sure, but it was a start, and it allowed Derek to leave his corporate job and join me full-time at the museum.

———

We've talked money in—what about money out? Every business has expenses, from envelopes to expensive capital purchases like equipment or real estate. Expenses are going to happen, and that's where paying attention to cash flow pays off. One of our biggest projects almost broke us because I wasn't looking close enough at the cash flow. We raised hundreds of thousands of dollars to produce a major outdoor exhibition. It was more money than we had ever seen, and it lulled me into a false sense of security. For these big projects, you raise a lot, but you spend a lot as well. After the opening celebration, I sat down the following Monday to check things off my to-do list, including paying everyone. Our vendors needed to be paid, and the various design teams we collaborated with needed their reimbursements. We had raised so much money that I didn't even think about it. I probably wrote twenty checks that day, without even looking at our bank account. Why would I? We were doing great!

About a week later, I realized what I did wrong, and I hope you don't repeat this mistake. Yes, we had raised a few hundred thousand dollars, but we didn't actually have it all. We had agreements signed and invoices sent, which are great but really worthless when it comes to actually paying your bills. As our vendors and design teams began cashing their checks that week, I watched our balance plummet, and I panicked. This mistake was going to bankrupt us.

One night, my wife Nicole came back to our loft and couldn't find me. I was so depressed and panicked, I laid down, fully clothed, in the dry bathtub with the lights turned off. I needed time to think, and this was my make-shift version of sensory deprivation. At the sight of me, Nicole started panicking. After she calmed down, I told her what happened, and she gave me some great advice: talk to the board. When I brought Scott up to speed, he did what he always did. He smiled and got to work helping me work the problem.

We couldn't recall the checks, as that would be bad form, but we could work to accelerate payment from the sponsors and donors who owed us on our invoices. Some of our sponsors were already months late paying us. I came to learn that very few companies pay on time, so why was I always so punctual? Companies sometimes delay payments to generate positive cash flow. With a few strongly worded—but not desperate—emails, we began hearing from folks. "Oh, I've been meaning to send this check," or, "I'll get on it with accounts payable and get you guys paid."

Cash flow is the movement of cash through your business. It's often called the lifeblood of business, but I prefer to think about it as a flow of water. Imagine a big jug of water, like one for serving people at a large outdoor event. It has an opening top and a spigot with a valve at the bottom. Water pours into the top (that's your revenue pouring into your bank account). When you have an expense, say to pay a bill or compensate a vendor, you open the valve on the spigot, and water (your cash) flows out. The amount of water that's in the jug at any given time is your working capital (the money you need to run your business day to day, month to month). Water flows through this system, just like cash flows through your business. You need enough working capital at any given time to cover your expenses as they come in and money needs to flow out. After the cash-flow crisis that had me laying in the dark in the bathtub, I began tracking cash flow like a hawk. Here's how I did it.

I started a very simple spreadsheet, broken down vertically by month, with a space under each month to add transactions. The column headings were Transaction Name, Credit, Debit, Balance, and Notes. I captured as many transactions, in and out, as I could in this spreadsheet. Credits made the balance go up, debits made it go down. The balance was our working capital in the bank. For example, if we received a $5,000 sponsorship from a design firm, I'd enter the name of the firm and $5,000 as a credit, and the balance would increase. Then say I had a bill for a service, $900, I entered that as a debit, and the balance would decrease. The notes column allowed me to put some detail for later—in some ways, this became a transaction journal.

Why not use accounting software like Quickbooks for this? I found Quickbooks too constraining, compared to my very editable spreadsheet. We used Quickbooks for accounting, but I needed a more malleable tool. I was only putting in transactions as they actually happened—not when I invoiced a sponsor, but when I actually deposited the money. Everything on this spreadsheet was real. So at any given time I knew the reality of our cash-flow situation and could make decisions based on it. I'm not exaggerating when I say I looked at this spreadsheet every night in bed on my phone, every morning, and I had it open throughout the day at work. In many ways, I became obsessed with cash flow—you should, too.

Over time, I realized I could use this tool to start predicting cash flow and cash needs. Many of our expenses were fairly predictable monthly expenses (things like payroll, web services like Dropbox, and rent). I knew with some reasonable certainty the dates within each month when these expenses would hit our account, so I loaded them into the future months, italicized these future expenses, and saw the impact on our balance. This was a little scary because I could see that these expenses would eventually drive our account to zero over a couple of months. This was a real-time view of our runway. I could tell you the exact date we would run out of money.

Runway, usually measured in months, is how much time you have left before your cash runs out, not taking into account the fact that, yes, you will generate more revenue. But what if you didn't? If you stopped generating cash, how long would you last? A month? A week? Knowing our runway was very motivating for me. When I saw in my cash-flow spreadsheet that we would likely run out of cash in 2 months, I would double or even triple my time focused on fundraising efforts.

I also used this spreadsheet as a forecasting tool for revenue. There were some revenue transactions I knew we could count on with 99% certainty. For example, when a board member committed to their annual giving, there was usually a 99% chance they would follow through. I knew when in each month these gifts would come in, so I loaded them into the spreadsheet, italicizing the text and numbers in the rows to denote they were future transactions. We also had annually recurring and monthly recurring revenue from membership. I knew how much would come in each month, so I lumped that revenue into aggregate future transactions. This extended our runway—with 99% certainty.

I used this spreadsheet as a living breathing model of my business. I would run what-if scenarios in there. What if we hired another staff person? I would add their payroll expense in each month for 12 months ahead to see how it affected cash flow over an extended period of time. What if we secured a big grant? What would that do to cash flow? Would it be worth it to apply? The answer was usually yes. In my MBA program, my professors would often say that as you build your business, you start to see the numbers in your mind. Working in this cash-flow spreadsheet every day—really, every hour—allowed me to see my business in my mind's eye.

I can't say that we never had a cash-flow crisis again. We did. There were times when I didn't pay myself in order to reduce expenses and extend cash flow. (I never missed paying my employees, though. Not once.) But I can say we never entered a cash-flow crisis that I couldn't see a mile away and take steps to mitigate before it got out of control. That was the power of this level of cash-flow modeling.

How much runway is enough? For thirteen years, I had a goal to have six months of runway and six months in cash reserve. What's a cash reserve? Remember our jug of water? Imagine you have another jug, and you can move water over to it, and it just sits there waiting, just in case you run out of your main, working capital, water. Six months of working capital runway and six months of cash reserve might have been unrealistic, but it comes down to your own risk tolerance. For the first ten years of the Design Museum, we ran with about one month of runway at any given time. That means we were always one month from going out of business.

As a young entrepreneur with no dependents, that was fine, though it drove me a little crazy at times. We'd get close to zero, and then Derek or I would secure a big donation or sponsorship, and boom, we were back in the game. As my life changed, and Nicole and I had kids, my risk tolerance changed. I wanted more security for myself and the museum, so I pushed to generate more working capital in the bank and started setting money aside in a cash reserve. Ironically, it was the COVID-19 pandemic and the capitalization that came from programs like the Paycheck Protection Program and the Economic Injury Disaster Loan that pushed up our cash on hand and allowed us to achieve runways as much as six months to a year at times—a much healthier place to be as a business.

In his book, *Profit First: Transform Your Business from a Cash-Eating Monster to a Money-Making Machine,* author Mike Michalowicz lays out a system for organizing and controlling cash flow. His system takes into account human nature—more specifically, entrepreneurs' nature to play it close to the edge, spending too much to grow their business and forgetting to generate a profit that allows them to live the lifestyle they're working so hard for.

In this model, Michalowicz has a table of percentages that defines which portions of revenue should be put toward profit, owner's pay, taxes, and operating expenses. Here's how it works. Instead of one bank and one account, you have two banks and six accounts. Cash from revenue flows into your income account. Every two weeks, you split that revenue into your other accounts based on set percentages that the author recommends. You transfer, say, 5% into your profit account, 50% into your owner compensation account (this is your paycheck), 15% into your tax account (you're going to need this later to pay taxes), and 30% into your operating expense account. Your operating expense account is the account you use to pay bills and keep your business going.

See the magic? You're taking profit and owner compensation out of the equation before you even pay expenses—you're taking the profit first. And now you're running your business on 30% of your cash from the start. Those other two accounts at the other bank come into play to truly protect you from spending. One is a parking spot for your profit, the other a holding pen for your taxes. You put them at another bank so you literally cannot see them when you log into your working capital bank. Out of sight, out of mind, until you want to use the profit for something, say a bonus or a trip, or until Uncle Sam wants his take, and you need to pay your taxes. The system takes work, but to me, it's worth the extra effort to hack the entrepreneur's natural tendency to use all or most of your cash to grow versus to pay yourself and build profit.

CHAPTER 11

Beyond Comfort Zone Momentum

Time for a big swing.

"Go big, or go home. Otherwise, you're wasting your youth."
—Jack Ma, co-founder, Alibaba Group

The team achieved some important milestones—the Design Museum was finally our focus. We had full-time employees, a few contractors, and interns. We had an office and fabrication facility. We were poised to take on our biggest project yet. In Chapter 8, we discussed how a solid brand, a brand that's more advanced or sophisticated than you are today, can pull you to the place you want to be. The same is true of a big project. A project that pulls you outside your comfort zone as an organization can pull you into the future and help create a new comfort zone that's bigger and better than before.

For the Design Museum team, that was just how we operated. Every project was bigger than the last. Whether it was an event series or an exhibition, we always took it to the next level. And we operated in full view of the public. We said what we were going to do, and then we did what we said, every single time. We believed that everything must build on the last thing we achieved—and with that attitude, you're never done, and you're never satisfied with the status quo. Our big project, the one that truly put us on the map, came from multiple strong collaborations. It all started with receiving the National Endowment for the Arts *Our Town* grant to explore placemaking strategies in Boston's Innovation District.

One of the most important parts of placemaking is listening to the community—so my first order of business was connecting with residents and businesses of the Fort Point and Seaport communities. I met with over 100 individual community, civic, and business leaders across the arts, startup, civic, corporate, retail, restaurant, and real estate communities. My objective was to embed myself in the needs and desires of this place. These individual meetings built up to a series of larger town halls where we introduced the Design Museum, the grant, and the high-level project goals to the broader community—and then we sat back and listened to their questions and ideas. A consistent thread we heard through all our one-on-one and town hall meetings was the desire from every community to activate the Fort Point Channel. The City of Boston even had a *Fort Point Channel Watersheet Activation Plan*, which codified a high-level vision for what could happen there.

The Fort Point Channel started as an inlet of Boston's inner harbor and, through the decades, was shaped by human efforts into an industrial waterway in the early 1900s. Over time, as the city became less about shipping and heavy industry, the channel lost its business use and became part of the fabric of the Fort Point neighborhood. When the Harborwalk was created, it curved down and around the long Fort Point Channel coast. And the channel's Harborwalk got an upgrade during the Big Dig when Massachusetts buried Interstate-93 underground to create the Greenway, and part of the highway was submerged under the Fort Point Channel. The stage was set for more public uses, and the community wanted more because they could see the potential of this beautiful body of water sitting on their doorstep. *The Fort Point Channel Watersheet Activation Plan* stated that the channel's watersheet was the same surface area as Boston Common, one of the oldest public parks in the country. It outlined the city's desire to turn the Fort Point Channel into Boston's next great public park. Here was our opportunity to use design to meet an opportunity and create place—to show how creativity could make an impact in a community.

At the same time, we were in discussions with the new leaders of the Boston Industrial Designers Society of America chapter about building a collaboration. Now run by Mario Gonzales and Jeremy Ogg, the chapter was in good hands and produced a really neat snow sled competition where local design firms designed sleds and competed in various challenges down ski slopes at a nearby mountain resort. They asked me to judge, and it was a blast—it was so much fun to see everyone's creativity and then see the sleds in action. As we were brainstorming another competition to collaborate on, we kept coming back to the Fort Point Channel as a place and context for creativity. What if we could unleash the power of Boston's creative community on making the Channel into a public park?

That question, and lots of ideation, led us to the idea of a public bench design competition, the winners of which would be fabricated and installed around the Fort Point Channel. The idea utilized what I called a breadcrumb strategy. Most people simply walked across the bridges spanning the channel, missing the opportunity and beauty of the Harborwalk. We wanted to get people walking around the channel, so placing nicely designed benches at various points would get folks exploring, you'd be able to see the benches from the bridges, seek them out, and then get curious about seeing the next bench on the breadcrumb trail.

Street Seats was born. The vision was to hold an international design competition to design new, unique public benches for around the Fort Point Channel. Why public benches? First, they are fairly elemental to city life, and everyone knows what a bench is. They're simple, but you can get very creative with how they look and feel. Our only constraint was that the benches must seat two people comfortably. This would be a fully interactive exhibition. We didn't want to make design that you just look at; we wanted folks to be able to see and touch and interact with each bench.

Our vision for the program mapped to our funding model for it. The seed funding would come from the National Endowment for the Arts grant, but the real opportunity came from partnering with local businesses and landowners around the channel. We found sponsors for each bench based on location. And the sponsors got to keep their bench at the end of the exhibition, to either permanently install somewhere outside or move it (like to the lobby of their building). And it was first come, first serve, so there was a bit of scarcity, even if sponsors didn't actually know what their bench would look like till after the competition. If you were first to sponsor, you would get the first choice from the pool of benches.

Remember those naysayers from Chapter 4? Well, they were here, too. When I spoke to some leaders around the neighborhood, they let me know that what we were trying to do was impossible. The city would never permit this, and no one would allow these benches on their property. So many people I spoke to were jaded about anything creative or interesting happening in public in Boston. But our magic answer was that these benches would be temporary. We would return each site to its original condition when the outdoor exhibition was complete—almost as if they were never there, so what was the risk? Also, I made sure to call it an outdoor exhibition, and not a bench installation project. We weren't installing benches. We were featuring temporary public art.

Our board fell in love with this big vision and jumped in to help secure sponsors and make this as big as we could. One of our board members, Chris Rowan, knew that public relations and press would be essential in getting maximum public attention—he introduced us to and helped us engage a pro bono PR strategist, Ruth Davis. Ruth was instrumental in getting the word out, not only in Boston but around the world. The same day as our membership launch party, Ruth lined up an outdoor press conference for us to announce *Street Seats* for the first time. We invited the press, potential sponsors, and community leaders to attend.

There on the Harborwalk, overlooking the Fort Point Channel, Derek and I shared our vision for *Street Seats: Reimagining the Public Bench,* a months-long public design program to activate the area around the Fort Point Channel with new designs, public events, and educational programming for kids. Folks were skeptically impressed and ready to see us succeed… or fail. We were a small team, and this was a huge project. If we could pull it off, we could prove we were a player in the Boston cultural landscape, signaling to our audience and funders that we were the real deal. We were going to do it, no matter what, because doing what you say you're going to do is all you have at the end of the day when you're a small startup.

We launched the international competition and fundraising effort without an official permit from the City of Boston to do the project—but we were confident we would figure it all out in parallel.

We created two foundational documents and corresponding web pages to get the word out. Like all our programs, we created a sponsor packet that laid out all the details of the project. I even did a photorealistic rendering of what one of the benches could look like along the channel and illustrated a high-level schedule of what would happen when and how sponsors could integrate into the program. Sponsorships ran from a few thousand dollars to tens of thousands. Sponsors received visibility throughout the program including on our beacon signage next to their sponsored bench. Our beacons were very prominent educational and wayfinding signage next to each bench—they were eighteen inches square by about six and a half feet tall. Each side contained information about the program, the museum, and the bench, its designer, or its design team. The beacons created a nice mini-billboard opportunity for sponsors to place their logo, proudly supporting good design in Boston.

We met with property owners, corporations, and local businesses to pitch sponsorship. There was a lot of interest— folks were excited to host a bench on their property and, ultimately, own it—scarcity and first-mover dynamics came into play as folks wanted to be one of the twenty bench sponsors, and they wanted to have the first pick of which bench they received. There was still some skepticism as to whether the City of Boston was going to allow this. I confidently assured them that we had all the necessary approvals—but we didn't. At least, not yet. My confidence came from the fact that if the property was owned privately, say by a company or a person other than the city, they could pretty much do what they wanted in terms of seating on their property. It was the city-owned land, like the sidewalks and Harborwalk, that had me worried.

The other fun thing for sponsors was they could nominate a judge from their organization, which helped mitigate the, "Which bench will I get?" worry since they would personally play a part in choosing which benches were chosen to be built full-scale. To offset a jury composed only of sponsors, we recruited design leaders from around the country to participate as judges, including designers from our Board of Directors and people like Steelcase Design Director Bruce Smith.

The other key documentation was the *Street Seats Challenge Call for Entries.* This similarly set the vision for the program, the overall schedule from an entrant perspective, key constraints on the design, including maximum sizes, and the entry requirements for each round of the competition. To enter the competition, designers or teams of designers had to submit a poster detailing their design using graphics, renderings, illustrations, and text, and they had to make and mail us a 1/8" scale model of their bench. The requirement for a scale model ended up being one of the smartest things we did on Street Seats since it mitigated the risk of getting shoddy benches. If you can build a nice model of a bench, you're more likely able to build a full-size, high-quality bench. And if you built a model, we knew you were serious about the project. These small physical models also afforded us an awesome exhibition opportunity.

We put the call for entries out into the world with the help of Ruth Davis, along with press releases, story pitches, social media posts, and more. I find when you put this kind of creative vision and energy into the world, it gives it right back. We didn't need to wait long for the posts and articles to start popping up in publications around the world. We were getting attention, and our hope was that attention would translate into designers taking the leap and submitting a design.

There was, of course, a lull as folks everywhere were learning, absorbing, and deciding whether to engage, during which we questioned everything. It would take some time for designers to become aware of the competition and create their designs. But after a few weeks, we started receiving posters

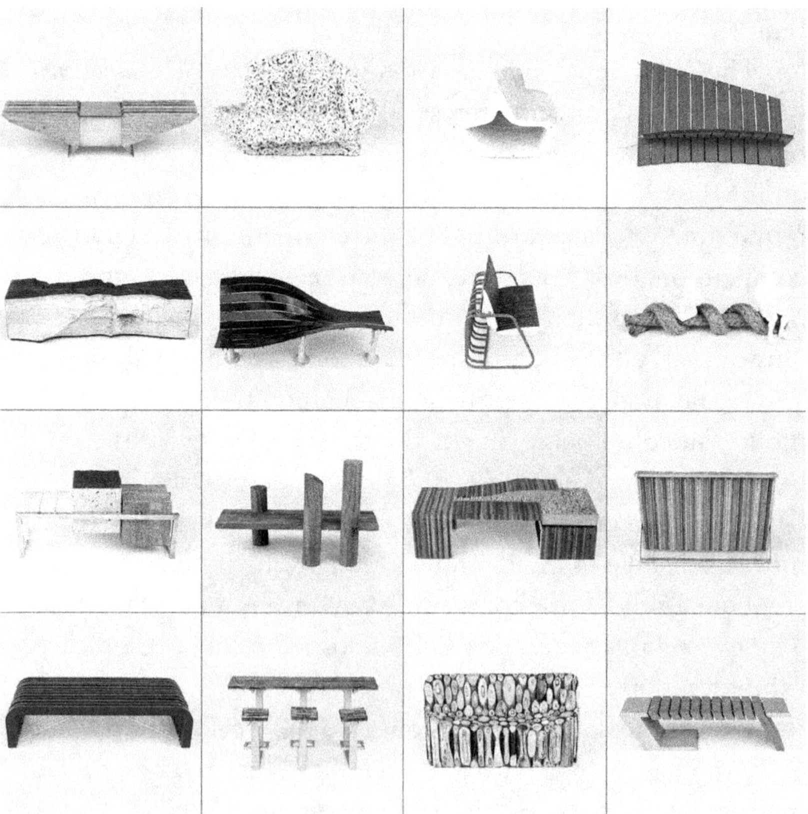

Scale models of Street Seats design entries.

through our digital entry platform—exciting! There was a deadline for competition registration and poster designs. Folks had a few more weeks to make and ship their scale model. When the scale models started to arrive, that's when it, quite literally, got very real.

Each little box that arrived was like a Christmas present for us. We opened each with care, documenting the model, confirming receipt, and generally marveling at the design ingenuity of our entrants. Our office became a little scale model park with all sorts of cool bench designs populating our dollhouse-sized little world. All told, we received close to 200 entries from twenty-three countries and twenty-two states within the U.S. We filled a gallery with the mini bench models for a special event and invited the community—and our judges—to see the benches for the first time. Hundreds showed up to get a glimpse of the bench designs. Imagine rows of shelves, each with unique bench designs, and each model had a QR code next to it so you could scan it with your smartphone and see the poster that went along with the model.

That night, the judges had the impossible task of choosing twenty semi-finalists to receive funding and fabrication mentorship in order to build their bench full-scale and have it installed as part of the outdoor exhibition. While our big community party went on, the judges sequestered in a nearby conference room with all the posters. After a lot of discussion and a few hours, they made their decision. That night, we announced the semi-finalists and handed out trophies to the winners. The exciting thing for us was that there was a really nice variety to the twenty semi-finalists—some from Boston, some from across the United States, and a few international winners. That night, they celebrated, but they still had a lot of work to do—now, they had just a few weeks to build a full-scale version of their bench, make a video, and gather all their sketches and design process materials for the exhibition beacons.

While all this fun creativity was going on, I was also doing something patently not creative: trying to get a city permit so we could actually pull this off in public. A standard permit simply didn't exist to temporarily install twenty public benches around the Fort Point Channel. I would visit the city permitting office a few times a week, wait in line, and then get another request denied, or a vague list of next steps. You have to imagine a dark, concrete, Boston City Hall room, with four permit clerks at a long, tall desk—so you're standing, but they're sitting—and behind them stacks and stacks of paper and folders, which I could only assume were all the permits in process, except mine. If there was a single computer in the place, I couldn't spot it. Behind the imposing desk, four sentinel clerks, the tables and shelves full of paper, and another concrete wall sat the actual decider.

Sadly, I never made it to her—I never actually got a city permit to install the benches around the channel. But that doesn't mean I stopped. Once again, our connections came through. I went right back to Randi Lathrop and Kristin Phelan at the Boston Redevelopment Authority and pleaded my case. They had seen the bench model gallery and saw first-hand the community's reaction to the creative work we were doing. I let them know I was concerned about the risk of moving forward with the project and public installation on city property without a permit. I didn't want the design teams spending their precious time and resources to make a bench, get it to Boston, install it, and then watch a city maintenance crew remove it within a week. They understood, and they were well aware of the challenges in getting public art permitted in the city—even as a city department, they had run into the same issues.

Permits for this kind of work simply didn't exist yet. So they gave me a different form—honestly, I don't know if they made this just for me or if this was something they gave to anyone struggling to get a permit for public art. It was a piece of paper with an area at the top to describe your project and a table below with sections for each city department that required approval with the name of the person you needed a signature from—think city engineer, city electrician, the fire department, police, and more. It was almost as daunting as going to the permit office over and over again, but at least with every signature I tracked down, I got closer to completing the form. In the end, I did it and acquired some cover for the designers working so hard to create their benches.

Over the next month or so, we worked closely with the designers to help them realize their visions as full-scale, publicly installable benches. The semi-finalists were required to deliver that full-scale bench, capable of seating two people and lasting for months (if not years) outdoors around the channel. They also needed to send in a design process video chronicling their design process, a written story, and as many images, sketches, and renderings as they could. The teams could deliver their benches to us at our fabrication facility bordering the Fort Point neighborhood by mid-April, or they could install their bench alongside us. The plan was to install the benches on April 23, 2013, and have a grand opening celebration and final judging next to the channel on April 27.

————

On April 15, 2013, my wife Nicole ran the Boston Marathon, just like every other year we were together. I drove her to Hopkinton for the start, then drove to various spots along the marathon route to cheer her on. We agreed I'd park our Jeep back at the apartment, then walk to meet her just past the finish line to help her get into a cab for a quick drive home. She finished the race and made her way through the medical area and the crowds on Boston Common. When I saw her, she had a big smile on her face. She had finished again! As I hailed a cab and got her into the back seat, I heard an explosion. We arrived home, and my first priority was Nicole. I got her some food and drink, and she wanted to get directly in the bathtub. As she soaked, I was on my phone. As I read the news, I dropped my phone and started crying.

Two explosions had rocked the Boston Marathon finish line. At that point, no one knew the full impact, but we learned later that three people were killed and over 250 were injured. We were in shock. Nicole had passed through the finish line, which was now chaos, less than thirty minutes prior. We were lucky. So many others were not, and the City of Boston was in a state of collective shock and mourning. We were glued to the news for the next week as stories from survivors and loved ones of those who were killed poured out. And the manhunt for the terrorists was on. On April 19, city officials shut Boston down. Everyone was meant to shelter in place the entire day as they closed in on the bombers. They caught the one surviving terrorist that night in Watertown, outside of Boston, and the situation came to a close. But our fear and shock weren't so easily tempered.

The Boston Marathon represented the best of what humanity is all about—people from all over the world coming together to push themselves and achieve greatness while supportive crowds cheer them on. We couldn't believe something like this could happen in our city, but the sadness for loved ones lost was very real. That Friday night, after they caught the bomber, Nicole turned to me and vowed to run the marathon again in 2014. She, like many others, wanted to show solidarity with the victims' families and the survivors.

It felt silly to think about this in the wake of so much change and tragedy, but where did all of this leave *Street Seats?* This was meant to be our biggest public program ever. Our team and designers around the world invested so much in making it all happen. Three days after the massive manhunt, we were supposed to install eighteen public benches around the Fort Point Channel, about a mile from the marathon finish line. There were some on our team and on the board who wanted to cancel or significantly postpone—how could we do this in the wake of the tragedy? Was it the right time? Derek and I and others wanted to push on, both in respect for all the creative work the designers had done, and also, potentially, as a way for the city to start to heal.

It was scary to think about bringing a few hundred people together in public, outside—should we hire security? Did we need to reconnect with Boston PD to make sure this was okay? The opening event was supposed to take place in a parking lot adjacent to the Fort Point Channel, owned by Gillette, so it was private property, but our tours would take large groups of people around the channel to the various bench locations. We confirmed with Gillette, and they were okay with us proceeding, so on April 23, less than a week after the bombing, we began installing the *Street Seats* benches.

Installation day was intense. We had the support of the Other Guys Moving Company and tons of volunteers— everyone was linked up with walkie-talkies, covering a few square miles. Derek lined it all up; he's so good at running things in the field. On the day of installation, benches were still being delivered, either at our office or directly to their location on the channel. We grouped teams by area and linked each with a moving truck from Other Guys. I made copies of that form with all the Boston government officials' signatures and gave them to everyone involved. Every volunteer had the form folded up in their pocket, so if someone tried to stop them and asked what they were doing, they could pull it out at a moment's notice. It wasn't a city permit, but it did look official.

Some designers and design teams elected to install their benches themselves. Andrew McClure shipped his fan-like bench from Paris and flew in that morning to pick up the boxes from our office and installed the bench himself along the channel. His bench was made of individual fins that locked together using a security cable that then anchored the bench in place. Another team from Dyer Brown Architects went extreme with their bench installation. During the day I received text messages from one of their designers to meet them on the Summer Street Bridge—they were driving their bench in and would install it themselves.

Waiting on the Summer Street Bridge, I saw a gigantic crane truck roll onto the little bridge, stop, and begin lowering its stabilizing feet. I started to sweat—we definitely didn't have a permit for a huge mobile crane—I didn't even know if the bridge could handle the weight. But there it went, extending its boom and lifting a concrete bench with a solar panel attached fifty feet into the air, and then setting it ever so lightly right in its spot on the sidewalk.

As we got all eighteen benches settled in, we also started installing our free-standing kiosks, our beacons, one next to each bench. One side of each beacon contained information about the Design Museum and one had a map of *Street Seats*, with a brochure holder containing maps folks could take with them. The other two sides were all about the benches. Derek used his amazing creativity and influence to make the beacons the stars of the *Street Seats* show.

As I've mentioned, Derek worked for Philips Color Kinetics, an outdoor commercial LED lighting manufacturer. Derek thought *Street Seats* was an amazing opportunity for Color Kinetics to showcase what they could do with colored LED lighting to make a unique outdoor experience. He convinced the managers there to sponsor *Street Seats*, not only financially, but with time, materials, and expertise as well. Derek designed the beacons to have an LED light fixture at the top—the kind that would normally grace the top of a skyscraper—which could produce any color. And they were bright. The beacons were wayfinding posts, you could stand at one end of the half-mile-long channel and see their multi-colored lights dotting the area and know that next to each was a really cool bench design to check out. The beacons united the entire outdoor exhibition and brought an exciting educational element as well.

One of the coolest things Derek did was connect the beacons to a mobile app that knew which bench you were standing next to and served you content like additional images and videos about that very bench. To do this Derek and the team at Philips needed to install a high-powered Wi-Fi network somewhere in the center of all the beacons. The logical spot was the top of the Tea Party Ship and Museum, a local historical attraction commemorating the Boston Tea Party.

Somehow, in the way only Derek could, he convinced the Tea Party Museum to let us install a powerful Wi-Fi transmitter at the top of their attic. With that Wi-Fi network blanketing the Fort Point Channel area, our *Street Seats* mobile web app could position you, so we knew which bench you were near, and the app could serve up relevant content. The app had another super cool feature: you could pull up a color wheel, and by dragging your finger across the colors, you could change the color of the beacon light. It was so fun and a great way for folks to interact with the exhibition and make it their own.

By this time, my wife Nicole and I were living in the Fort Point area—with its vibrant artist community and live/work studio space, it was perfect for her ceramics business. We went for walks on the channel every night to check on the benches. We would usually sit at one of the benches overlooking the whole channel. A little-known feature of the app was you could click on any bench beacon on the map, from anywhere, and change the light color. So at night, I would go fishing for people's attention. I'd see a couple walking past one of the benches, I'd select it on the app, pull up its color wheel, and make the beacon light go crazy, changing colors wildly. This would usually get folks' attention, they'd see the light, then they'd look down and see the bench. Voilà, a new person learning about design.

The installation looked amazing. The benches were gorgeous examples of design, each one unique in its design and construction. There was the *Knot Bench,* basically a bench formed by knitting in three dimensions, the *Bowsprit* and *Cleat,* both inspired by boating forms and materials, and the *Wave Bench,* which took its cues from the ocean. The beacons looked great as well—they were super fun and innovative, and we had

Father and son sitting on the Bowsprit bench, reading information on our beacon, 2013.
Photo: Diana Ye

our printed maps available on the beacons and at local businesses. We were ready to open this giant outdoor exhibition. But we still didn't know if people were ready to gather in public after the tragedy at the Boston Marathon.

The morning of the outdoor opening celebration, we all got set—we had a big day ahead. We had almost forty volunteers in orange design museum t-shirts, including my wife, my sister-in-law, and brother-in-law. We set up multiple tents on the Gillette parking lot to provide shade, and give attendees direction and a chance to vote on the people's choice award. Our twenty judges arrived early to walk around the exhibition and make their final determination on who would win the cash prizes. The judges received the first walking tour, after which we planned to give guided walking tours to small groups around the one-mile Harborwalk—these would all start and end in the parking lot. Just like during installation, everyone was connected via walkie-talkies—we were ready.

It was my job to take the judges around the exhibition and guide them as they made their final decisions on winners—meanwhile, Derek and the rest of the team stayed back and continued prepping for attendees to arrive. It was super fun to get the judging group back together after the initial semi-finalist judging event. These folks were some of our dedicated board members, sponsors, and notable Bostonians. They were impressed by the scale models at our gallery show, now they were simply blown away by all the full-scale benches. I didn't envy them having to choose a top winner and two runners-up.

As we made our way around the channel, the judges discussed each bench thoroughly, but there was nothing on the radio from Derek or the team. I was about a half-mile from the main site, and I was getting worried the event would be a bust, but I kept a strong, confident face for the judges—everything would be fine either way. As we finished the loop, we came through a small walkway tunnel (the Harborwalk sort of went under the old brick buildings bordering the channel). As we turned the corner around the building back to the Gillette parking lot, we saw it. The site was packed with people—over 2,000 people came out! I hadn't heard from Derek on the radio because they were simply swamped getting folks paired up with tour guides and getting the people's choice voting going—it was amazing!

It turned out that the street seats opening celebration was just what people needed, a chance to get out after the events of the previous week and the marathon. *Street Seats* was a way to celebrate the city and our global creative community. Some of the design teams came, too. All the Boston-based teams were there, as well as teams from Mexico, France, and states across

the US. We created something way bigger than ourselves—
way bigger than our team of four—bringing the international
design community together to create something beautiful.
Seeing our Design Museum team and volunteers, board
members, judges, and attendees all come together and having
everyone enjoy the fruits of the collective creative labor
reminded me and everyone else about the importance of
community and the power of design.

Street Seats put us on the map in Boston—not an easy thing
to do for a nomadic museum with no single space to call our
own. It was in the parking lot during the opening celebration
that Danielle Duplin asked me to speak about the Design
Museum in my first TEDx talk. As what that opportunity
could mean for us swirled in my mind, the judges finalized
their picks for the finalists, and my sister-in-law Elizabeth and
brother-in-law Edward finished tallying the votes for the
people's choice. In the end, the judges picked the *Bowsprit*
bench as the top design. Designed by graduate students
Christa Lee, Rui Chen, and Sanchit Mittalit from Georgia
Institute of Technology, it was so meticulously crafted from
metal and wood and resembled the hull of a modern ship
sailing the newly christened Fort Point Channel as a park
made of water. And the people's choice award went to *The
Chroma Bench*—the back of the bench was designed in such a
way that as you walked past it, the bench changed color, which
perfectly mirrored our colored beacon lights.

In thirteen years, two of my favorite Design Museum
photos were taken during *Street Seats*. One is a pair of little boys
in matching Boston Red Sox hats sitting on a bench called
TwoFold, which was a modern take on a kid's sized table and
chairs, which we placed adjacent to the Boston Children's
Museum. The boys are sitting on the bench looking into the

Brothers sitting on the TwoFold bench, 2013.
Photo: Diana Ye

Design Museum volunteers at the Street Seats Opening Celebration, 2013.
Photo: Diana Ye

distance with the channel waters behind them. The other is a photo of all forty of our volunteers, with their orange shirts on, all gathered on a walkway to a boat dock, smiling and proud of the work we had done together.

As the hours passed with music and chatting with friends and neighbors, the crowd began to dissipate. It really sunk in as Derek and I and the team did one last walk around the channel: we did it. We did what so many thought was impossible—not just impossible for a small team like us, but impossible for anyone to pull off in Boston. And we did it the right way. The city wasn't going to remove the benches after twenty-four hours. Months later, when it did come time to remove the benches and close the outdoor exhibition, the same city officials and neighborhood skeptics who said this was an impossible project asked if the benches could stay longer—many become permanent fixtures around the channel.

Street Seats brought vibrancy in a way that only creativity can—people walked the 1.5-mile exhibition throughout the day, they ate their lunches while sitting on the benches, and they came to our events where the designers spoke about their creations. It was a truly glorious seven months of design in Boston. The benches were so popular with children, we knew we had to do something for kids related to the show. When we were out on the site, walking the Harborwalk, we saw kids climbing all over the benches and generally loving the creativity around the channel.

We built on our relationship with the Boston Children's Museum. They had an existing weekend art program for kids, and we talked to them about moving it outside and making it all about bench design. We called it *Street Seats Kids.* Under a big tent every Saturday and Sunday, we gathered groups of kids for a tour around the channel. We gave them little booklets to do various activities like a scavenger hunt, and pages to sketch their favorite bench. When we made it back to the tent there were supplies for them to draw and build their own little bench model.

Something really fun we did was make a set of three six-sided dice that the kids would roll to get the design criteria for their bench. One die had six options for who the bench was for (yourself, your parents, your friends, your pet). The other had six options for the setting, (your backyard, the channel, your school). And the last one had six materials your bench should be made of (wood, metal, concrete). Rolling these dice helped make this less of an art project and more of a design problem to solve. The kids and parents loved it. We had crowds of kids every weekend, and, thankfully, we had the help of our orange-shirted volunteers to match.

On one of the kid-focused tours I led, I was walking the group around the exhibition trying to explain that each of the *Street Seats* benches was designed by a different group of people. At one point, we were walking past a classic Boston park bench. A sarcastic ten-year-old stopped us, pointed to the normal-looking wrought-iron bench, and said, "So Sam, I bet someone designed this bench, too, huh?" To all the kids' disbelief, I said, "Yes, a group of people designed this bench as well!" Their eyes widened. People just don't think about where the stuff around them comes from. I said, "Everything around you was designed by someone. Even the buildings." As the group of kids looked around the city, eyes wide with wonder, I said, "Yes everything is designed." That day, I achieved the mission of the Design Museum with that group of kids.

Street Seats was huge for us. It was a stretch project that took us outside our comfort zone and showed us what we were capable of. What's your stretch project? It could be trying to close a big account, one you're a little afraid to close because of what it might mean for your business. It could be launching that new product line or experimenting with a new business model. Don't be afraid to stretch—it might be just what you need to take you to the next level and find the operational state that brings you new customers, revenue, press, and more. *Street Seats* established our ability to do big, international, projects. We proved that we could do what we said we would do. Donors, sponsors, and partners could trust their time, money, and creativity with us—they knew our impact on the city and service to our community was real.

CHAPTER 12

Whatever it Takes

Wherever it takes you.

"Only those who will risk going too far can possibly find out how far one can go."
— T.S. Eliot, poet

At MassChallenge, we were fortunate to have a number of mentors to help guide us alongside our growing board of directors. One of our mentors was Ed Loessi, a marketing executive with a love of design. Ed is super smart and always gave us good advice on how we could take our model to the next level. One day in 2011, we were supposed to have a big combined board, mentors, and staff meeting to strategize about the months ahead. We were still working on our membership program and other monetization approaches, as well as thinking about our slate of programs to come.

The morning of the meeting, I received a few emails from folks saying they couldn't make it. As the meeting time approached, staff started to drop off, as well—everyone was busy and folks had other things going on. I got one last email from Ed asking if I still wanted him to come in, even if it was just going to be me and him. I remember thinking about it for a second but saying to myself, *I'll take as much time from any of our mentors as I can get.* If Ed was down to come over for a meeting to just chat openly about Design Museum strategy, I was going to soak it up.

So without an agenda, Ed and I met in one of the MassChallenge floor-to-ceiling glass corner conference rooms overlooking Boston Harbor. After the pleasantries, Ed asked me a question that would push my vision for the museum for years to come. He asked, "Where do you want to take this? What's your dream?" It was a big question to ask. We had not yet launched any kind of monetization, we were a tiny nonprofit with very little money in the bank, and we had no full-time employees. We were just trying to figure things out. But I'll say, that was a great time to talk about it person-to-person, entrepreneur-to-coach.

For a few months, I was sketching a map of the U.S., and putting dots on the major design-forward cities across the country. So I stood up in our conference room and drew the map on the whiteboard for Ed, complete with the dots for each city I dreamed we could scale the Design Museum model to over time. I explained to Ed that design truly is everywhere, not just in Boston—so why were we only focused on building community and educating the public here? Ed had a big grin on his face—I think this is exactly the conversation he wanted to have. With the right structure, we could scale our model to cities across the country, maybe even around the world, to create a truly distributed design museum that united our vision of accessible thought leadership across communities. I left the meeting energized. Ed thought it was possible—maybe it was?

————

We were constantly dreaming of how big we could go with the Design Museum, but as we grew, it was clear something was wrong with our team. I could tell Derek was frustrated, and maybe I was, as well. Admittedly, I was pushing really hard on all our programs, especially fundraising and *Street Seats*, to try to achieve some level of financial stability for the organization, grow our salaries, and even grow the team to increase our capacity and spread out the work amongst more staff. We were a team of five. Derek and I were full-time directors at $30,000/year. We had two full-time contractors, Jenna Casey on marketing, graphic design, and event production, plus Brynn Leggett, who focused on fundraising and grants. We also had a part-time contractor, Jenna Goldblatt, assisting on the *Street Seats* program as a project coordinator. We were a small team with big dreams—but maybe the dreams were too big.

Derek and I weren't as aligned as we normally were. The misalignment manifested in a few ways. We were both directors, but we had never really taken the time to divvy up responsibilities. In the early days, we were just both responsible for everything, but that was changing. We also started giving different directions to our team members and having separate conversations with the board, and sometimes the direction was conflicting and, therefore, confusing. When Derek and I discussed the situation, two things came into focus. Derek believed we were driving too hard to grow too fast. He asked me, "Why can't this just be you, me, and Jenna, making it happen? Why do we need more staff and more board members?" I knew where he was coming from. We were moving and growing so fast, but his question scared me as well. I didn't think we were pushing hard enough to grow. I was working on the museum around the clock, making $30,000 per year, which was barely enough to scrape by in Boston. I wanted the museum to be my career, maybe my life's work, but for that to happen, I needed a life! I couldn't work all the time. In my mind, we needed more money and more staff to make the museum and our lives everything I dreamed they could be.

The other thing that came into focus was the nature of our work. Derek and I were designers, and designers typically like to work on lots of different things, so to use our creativity, we sometimes shun sameness or rote process. But that's exactly what was happening at the museum. The design we were doing at the museum shifted. Prior to *Street Seats,* all our exhibitions looked different. Each had its own look and feel. *Creative Capital: Designed in Boston* leaned into illustrations of maps and cities like the Massachusestts map and the Boston skyline, with reds, greys, and white. *Getting There: Design for Travel in the Modern Age* had a totally different color palette of dark grey, golden yellow, bright sage green, and cobalt blue, with flat silhouette illustration styles and a focus on photography and images.

Looking at both examples without the aid of the introduction panel, which had our logo on it, how many people actually knew that one museum did both exhibitions? The different looks probably would have been fine if all our exhibitions were in the same place. A traditional museum has that going for it—an overall institutional brand and the benefit of having you physically in their own building. But we were putting these exhibitions in other organizations' buildings.

This hit me hard twice in the span of a few months. Remember *Retail: Retell. Recycle, Rethink,* the exhibition at Prudential Center Mall in collaboration with our students at Wentworth Institute of Technology? The exhibition was gorgeous, with great content and beautiful illustrations and photography. I loved to sort of lurk as other people checked it out, and, yes, I eavesdropped a bit. I heard one person say, "This is such a great exhibition that the mall put on." The mall? A thirty-foot version of our logo was plastered on the floor, but it didn't matter. The strength of being at the mall overwhelmed our brand.

The same happened when we installed *Getting There* at Grand Circle Gallery. I overheard someone say, "Grand Circle Gallery always produces such wonderful exhibitions." We had a problem here. Without the sense of place that a building provides, we weren't getting credit or brand alignment on our work. I theorized that we needed to standardize the design, brand, and color palette of our exhibitions, so no matter where they were installed you would know, without a doubt, that you were in a Design Museum Boston exhibition.

That was the project brief I gave our design intern, Joe Bradford, one of our amazing Wentworth students. Joe came up with two things that would shape our exhibitions for the next decade. First, he identified a standard exhibition building method using the products from a company called Esto, plastic connectors and square aluminum tubing. Esto basically makes a building kit for trade shows, and Joe's idea was to turn around and use these materials for modular museum exhibitions. We could build anything out of it, displays, pedestals, signage, anything. Joe also came up with what he coined "The Doticon." The Design Museum logo is made up of around 300 dots. In Joe's mind, each dot represented a public program we were doing. We were just too zoomed out to see the detail of each dot. He designed an orange dot with a white icon for each program. Dot plus icon equals doticon. So our exhibitions would have our logo, our color palette (the strong design museum orange, dark red, dark brown, and white), and they would each have their own unique doticon. For *Getting There*, it was a plane taking off. For *Creative Capital*, it was the state of Massachusetts with a star over Boston. For *Retail*, it was a retail tag. For *Street Seats*, it was an illustration of a typical park bench in white within an orange dot.

In my mind, we were maturing as an organization and operationalizing our design work to fix a problem in the marketplace. But I understand what it meant for Derek. He wanted to be a designer, designing new products, graphics, everything—and our need for unique design was diminishing as we established a strong, repeatable design language and fabrication system. The museum turned into a business design challenge filled with management, operations, and financial challenges to design for—which I loved and thrived in.

Looking back now, though, I realize I didn't make a lot of space for Derek to explore his creative practice in that realm. I was hyper-focused on building this business, and I was leaving my co-founder behind. We knew we wanted different things, and we agreed that no matter what happened, our friendship was more important than any business, even our museum. Once again, we did what we did best: we asked for help. Both of us built a strong relationship with Scott Reilly over the years —we both trusted him. Scott agreed to act as an advisor and mediator as we figured out our next steps together. We each spoke with Scott at length, multiple times, and then spoke with him together, as well. It was hard but necessary to achieve a good result.

In the end, Scott had a brilliant idea. Derek wanted to move on from the museum and pursue more design opportunities, but he didn't want to leave his baby behind. I wanted to step up into an Executive Director role, but I didn't want to lose Derek as a business partner and certainly didn't want to lose him as a friend. Scott's solution was elegantly simple, Derek could leave the staff and join the board of directors. He could still be involved, but he was also able to go to the next step in his career. I became the Executive Director of Design Museum Boston, and Derek would become one of my managers, as the board collectively oversees the work of the Executive Director.

I'll never forget the day Derek made it official. It was a beautiful day, and he suggested we go for a walk through the marine industrial park. As we made our way to the ocean, we talked about how much we accomplished together—it was a real trip down memory lane. We reached the ocean and sat on the edge of a pier talking about what was next for both of us. Derek was going to join the board and had a job offer to design toys at Hasbro, something he always wanted to do. I shared with him where I was thinking about taking the museum next. Our friendship was intact (and still is) thanks to Scott and the effort we put into communicating and problem-solving.

As our conversation on that pier ended, we sat in silence—a rare thing for the two of us—until the sky opened up in a torrential downpour. As we ran through the rain back to the office laughing, I couldn't help but think this was the perfect metaphor for our last four years together, sprinting to make the Design Museum happen. Despite everything, we built it together, and we had so much fun. Derek planned to stay on through the *Street Seats* project and join the board later in the year. It wasn't ideal. I would come to miss my co-founder very much as the years went on, but change is inevitable.

———————

The attention from *Street Seats* not only put us on the map in Boston, but it made my dream of scaling the Design Museum across the country feel more possible. During the run-up to *Street Seats*, I must have met with every community leader in the Fort Point area. So when two consultants from Portland, Oregon, were touring the neighborhood and looking for creative placemaking partners, someone must have told them about me, Derek, and Design Museum Boston. Ann Edlen and Ann Hudner—who I would come to affectionately call "The Anns"—were representatives of Gerding Edlen, a real estate development company that was preparing to develop a handful of residential properties in the Fort Point neighborhood. Gerding Edlen was a unique developer that focused not only on developing buildings but also cared deeply about sustainability and community.

At our first meeting, Ann, Ann, Derek, and I talked for hours about design and placemaking, and we all became fast friends. It was clear we shared the same values around the power of design, the importance of community, and the power of place. Almost overnight, Gerding Edlen became one of our biggest sponsors and partners. They sponsored and hosted some of our *Design Museum Mornings* events focused on creative placemaking. Ann's son Matt—a partner at the development firm—even spoke at one, weaving design, real estate, environmental sustainability, and community engagement into a dynamic talk that perfectly set up our *Street Seats* program in the neighborhood. Matt went on to be a judge on *Street Seats*, and Gerding Edlen sponsored a bench design. The Anns also commissioned us to develop, curate, and install an exhibition in the community space of one of their new buildings. We called the exhibition the *Urban Innovation Gallery* and featured examples of local art, design, and technology innovations being developed in the Fort Point area.

Eventually, and organically, we asked the Anns to join our board of directors. And that was just about the same time I started floating the idea of national expansions at our board meetings. My initial idea was simple: design is everywhere, not just in Boston, so why only focus on being nomadic in one city? I spoke about the power of our brand; the infrastructure we were building, including traveling exhibitions; how economies of scale and local community fundraising in cities around the U.S. could take us to the next level. Some of the board was intrigued enough to keep talking about it. They asked what cities I had in mind. I was ambitious, but not crazy. My original plan was to attempt to scale by expanding to Providence, R.I.—a city less than an hour from Boston and one to which many of us, including Derek, the board, and myself, had many connections. The Anns were at these meetings, and I could easily tell that they had a different city in mind.

The Anns had an interesting idea and an ask of Derek and me. They wanted to bring us to Portland, Oregon, to present at the upcoming Pacific Northwest College of Art (PNCA) board meeting. Ann Edlen also sat on and led the PNCA board as chair, and she wanted us to share our unique story and approach to activating the Boston creative community. Providence was an hour away, and Portland was across the country—but I couldn't help but think about that meeting with Ed Loessi where I drew the map of the U.S. with dots on all the cities that Design Museum could be in. We agreed to the trip and visited Portland in late January 2013, just weeks after we officially hired ourselves as full-time employees of the museum.

Ann Hudner is one of the smartest strategists I know, and she had a plan to authentically introduce us to the entire Portland design community at every level—community organizations, business leaders, media, and more. Derek and I presented to the PNCA board. We had lunch with design leaders at Wieden+Kennedy. We had breakfast with design community leaders at ADX, a unique maker space in town, and toured academic institutions. Ann even got the press involved—we were interviewed by local design bloggers and Portland Monthly magazine. The Anns were introducing us to Portland, but just as importantly, they were introducing Portland to us. And it worked. I saw the parallels between the key characteristics that defined the design community in Boston right before we launched the museum—the same things were happening in Portland, as well.

Portland was on the cusp of rapid urban change, and the creative community was lining up to coalesce as a real force. I started speaking at length with Ann Hudner about the possibility of expanding the Design Museum. I was still thinking about Providence as a safe bet, but Ann was part of an informal group trying to bring the creative community together in Portland to elevate the city as a creative center at a critical time in the city's growth. She knew I wanted to expand the museum across the country, so she played to my ambition. She asked, "Do you want to be a regional organization, or do you want to be national?" And, of course, I wanted to be national. Being bi-coastal would be a great position from which to kick off a nationwide expansion to other major cities between Boston and Portland across the U.S.

In the midst of planning for *Street Seats,* I made another trip to Portland that spring to meet with potential donors and sponsors and craft my expansion pitch to the board. I presented my expansion proposal to the board at our June 2013 board meeting, hoping for a vote of approval that would make the expansion real. This was one of the most important pitches I've made in my career and I felt like I used every bit of design and business knowledge I had accumulated through all my experiences. The pitch started high-level: design is everywhere was our slogan, so we knew acutely that design is in more cities than just Boston. And based on our model, as a museum without a building, we weren't going to be able to go deep into one market—that would mean getting a building and going the traditional route. If we weren't going to do that, I posited, then we needed to go wide as a nomadic, distributed museum operating in multiple markets.

Traditional museums have a lot going for them in terms of funding. They portray a sense of permanence to funders. They literally have roots, foundations in the ground that solidify their buildings and their place in the community. They may be inaccessible and have high operating costs, but they are certainly permanent. As such, they can put people's and companies' names on things, like on the outside of the building, on plaques around the spaces, and on exhibitions—museums have even started naming bathrooms to recognize major donors. One visit to the Museum of Science Boston and you don't need to look closely at all. Everything has someone's name on it—everything is named because everything is supported by a person or organization.

As a nomadic museum without a building, we don't control the spaces we exhibit in. And try as we did with our strong brand, our ever-present traveling programming, and online presence, for some donors, especially back in 2013, we didn't seem like a permanent bet for their money. There were people supporting us though, folks who believed in our mission and were innovative in their thinking on how a museum could operate in the 21st century. We needed to find more of those people, which meant searching for them in more markets. I wanted to grow the pond we were fishing in.

The same idea rang true for membership. I wanted to grow our opportunity to convert audience to membership, and entering a new city would introduce the museum to a whole new audience. My gut, and experience in Boston, centered on my feeling that there's a strong desire by many donors and foundations to support local organizations. So I didn't simply want to rename Design Museum Boston and be a national organization called, say, Design Museum America. I felt that if we wanted the same kind of engagement, support, and involvement we garnered from our community in Boston, we needed to be Design Museum Boston in Boston and Design Museum Portland in Portland to activate local support.

I pitched the idea of economies of scale—the idea that the larger we were, the more efficient we could be with our scarce resources and our intellectual property. For example, we pour hours of work and tens and hundreds of thousands of dollars into our exhibitions. We might pop that exhibition up once or twice in Boston. But what if we traveled that asset to other cities? A robust traveling exhibition market already exists in the museum world. Museum A raises money, develops an exhibition, and maybe makes some money on it, but the real money comes when they rent it out to other museums. Each rental is almost pure revenue since the costs of developing the exhibition are already complete. My thought was we could create our own traveling exhibition market. New exhibitions would be a high cost in the originating city, say Boston, but then each subsequent instance in other cities would be low cost. The margin is much larger for each instance than it is for the original. The idea was to turn our programs into assets that we would raise money for in each city and travel around the U.S.

Ultimately, I pitched the idea of spinning up a national organization, something like Design Museum America or Design Museum Network. I didn't have the perfect name, but I didn't let that stop me from making the pitch. This parent organization would be the umbrella structure for the first two branches, Design Museum Boston and Design Museum Portland. This was akin to the public library system. You have your main branch, and then the local branches—they're all part of the same system. We would have nationally focused staff, doing things like finance and operations, grant writing, design, exhibition development, etc., and locally focused staff doing events, community building, and local fundraising from members, donors, corporate sponsors, and foundations in specific cities.

I pitched the business plan and the strategy, and I asked the board to put my proposal to a vote. Derek was still going to be on staff for another eight days, so he wasn't yet on the board and couldn't vote. But I could tell that this pitch and new approach were part of the reason he wanted to move on. I know it was aggressive. We were small. We had just completed our biggest project to date with *Street Seats,* and we really had to stretch to make it happen. I know Derek and some of the board members were thinking, "How the hell is this small team going to pull this off?"

There was another group of board members who thought my pitch and this post-*Street Seats* moment was the perfect chance to become a traditional museum. In their minds, being nomadic was a way to get started, and launching something like *Street Seats* meant we were ready to pivot again. We did it, we were started up, and our big programs proved we could do it—they thought it was time to get a building and establish ourselves as the leading design museum in New England.

After laying out the pitch, all the arguments and plans, and answering everyone's questions, silence filled the room. Everyone knew it was time to make a decision, and this was a turning point for our company. I'm terrible at awkward silences, so in these moments at board meetings, and at this particular meeting, I blurted out, "Okay, now it's time to vote." I don't begrudge anyone their thoughts on the pitch or how they voted.

It was kind of a crazy proposal when I think about it now. I know I was a bit naive, but you need to be a bit naive, or you won't get out of bed in the morning. A board member asked how much money I would need to invest to get a new city off the ground. I naively said $3,000. That was enough to get a microphone, a PA system, some pop-up signs, and some brochures. I was confident, and dead wrong, by a factor of ten (if not 100). If I knew everything it was going to take to really establish Design Museum Portland at that moment, I probably would have curled into a little ball and quit. A little bit of not knowing can be a good thing.

The board slowed me down and deliberated, first with us in the room, then they asked Derek and me to step out. Then they called us back in to talk some more. In the end, they all agreed that this big of a decision should be a unanimous decision, so two board members abstained from the vote. The rest of the group voted to approve. I was elated—I felt this scaling strategy in my bones, all the way back to drawing the map of the U.S. on the whiteboard in my meeting with Ed Loessi. This was the way to make a nomadic museum work—being nomadic in one market would be a crawl to build a sustainable business. Being a nomadic museum in multiple markets would allow us to grow and achieve financial stability.

I didn't get to celebrate for too long, though, because the minute the unanimous vote was recorded, the two board members who abstained resigned their board seats on the spot. One of them was my mentor, Scott Reilly, who taught me so much about fundraising and the museum world overall. Scott was interested in helping to build a strong museum in Boston, not a national organization. But in my mind, our business model just wouldn't work in one city. National expansion was our future. The board vote to approve my proposal kicked off our national focus and a ton more work and learnings. We expanded to Portland, OR, bringing together an amazing design community there and linking our communities in Boston and Portland. We didn't stop there. We curated, designed, and launched a number of nationally traveling exhibitions and events that we produced in Chicago, San Francisco, Las Vegas, Dallas, Seattle, and more.

Once again, betting big pulled us into the future and set us up to grow our brand and audience nationwide, even worldwide—and all of this pushed me and the team to continue honing our ever-growing operation. It wasn't easy, but big things usually aren't. What big swings are unique to your business model? Maybe you never go for the level of scale we were aspiring to, but I recommend at least writing down some of your more crazy ideas to grow and scale—maybe some of them aren't so crazy. Pick an idea that can have a big impact, prototype it, analyze it, build a strategy, and then bet on yourself and your idea. Go big.

CHAPTER 13

Making it Happen, Every Day

Just keep swimming.

"Easy isn't the goal. Quality is the goal."
— Ed Catmull, co-founder, Pixar

With the success of *Street Seats,* we felt like we were gaining real traction. We were achieving what some call product-market fit, meaning that our business model, our approach, our product, and our audience were gelling. The system was working, we were scaling it, but after big swings like *Street Seats* and scaling to Portland, what was next for our business?

The founders of Pixar faced a similar moment. Pixar was founded in 1986 with the notion that computer animation was going to change the game. A decade and many innovations later, they were right—they launched the first feature-length computer-animated movie that we've all come to love, the original *Toy Story. Toy Story* was a big swing that paid off. But in the summer of 1994, as the company was putting the final touches on the film, the director, John Lasseter, and writers

Andrew Stanton, Joe Ranft, and Peter Docter went out to lunch, got to talking, and asked each other, "Well, what comes next?" Stanton recalled about the lunch conversation, "Toy Story was almost complete, and we thought, well geez, if we're going to make another movie we have to get started now." What followed was a conversation over lunch with idea sharing and napkin sketches that would generate nearly $1 billion in box office revenue.

At that one lunch at the Hidden City Café in Point Richmond California in 1994, Lasseter, Stanton, Ranft, and Docter sketched the outlines and characters that would become four of the studio's biggest movies, 1998's A Bug's Life, 2001's Monsters, Inc., 2003's Finding Nemo, and 2008's WALL-E. Stanton later acknowledge that, of course, many more people worked on, added ideas, and made the films successful. But one lunch, four successful movies. The team at Pixar had their product-market fit with *Toy Story*—they could feel that it was a game changer. Instead of resting on their laurels, they figured out how and what to keep delivering for their audience and how to keep taking things to the next level.[10]

———

That lunch might feel like magic, and maybe it was—but I felt that same magic from just one fateful meeting at the Design Museum. Similarly, we were taking our biggest swing yet with *Street Seats*. The program was well underway with the design competition and gallery show—we knew it was going to be huge. I was wondering, *what's next after Street Seats? How do we*

———

10 Frank Pallotta, "How Napkin Sketches During A Pixar Lunch Meeting Led To Four Of The Studio's Greatest Movies," Business Insider, Apr 29, 2014, https://www.businessinsider.com/pixar-movies-thanks-to-napkin-sketches-at-lunch-meeting-2014-4/.

keep this momentum? My thought partner in all of this, Derek, was planning to leave the museum once *Street Seats* was open, so for the first time in a while, I felt alone in this work. But I wasn't alone. I had an amazing board of directors and community around me, so the most important thing I did was admit that I didn't have the answers, that I wasn't alone, and that I needed help.

I asked Derek and three of the board members I trusted the most in terms of audience engagement and programming, Scott Reilly, Sarah Morris, and David Silverman, to think about what came next. I created a document template that I called an *Idea Proposal* that had sections to fill in, nothing too fancy—things like title, description, how the idea fit our mission, who the audience was, how much effort it would take, etc. We set up our first programming committee meeting for early April 2013—two weeks before the big *Street Seats* outdoor opening celebration.

The five of us gathered at the Design Museum office for the evening meeting, and I could feel from the beginning it was going to be one of the most important moments in our history —everyone was buzzing with excitement to share their ideas. In that one meeting, we discussed six ideas for major exhibition and event programs that would keep us going for the next five years, positioning us as one of the premier outlets for design experiences, community, education, and impact.

Sarah proposed *Green Patriot Posters,* a traveling exhibition of posters designed to inspire the fight against climate change. Her brother Edward Morris and his partners were inspired by the propaganda posters of WWII, which were employed to inspire the fight against Nazis, and they worked with designers around the world to develop a collection of posters that similarly used graphic design to inspire change. They did some

Green Patriot Posters exhibition at 315 on A in Boston, 2014.

small exhibitions and even had a book, but Sarah knew that Edward and the team were looking for more opportunities to get the posters out into the world. This was a brilliant idea by Sarah. She knew we'd be pretty spent after *Street Seats,* and here was a collection of design work that was already curated. The organization was looking for a partner, and it fit our mission perfectly.

In January 2014, we launched a major traveling exhibition of *Green Patriot Posters* in Boston at 315 on A, a new Gerding Edlen Building—complete with large format posters, videos, and an interactive projection where visitors could browse the full collection of hundreds of posters. On the evening of the opening reception, Edward and I gave a tour to Boston's new mayor, Marty Walsh. Later that year, in August 2014, we brought the exhibition to Portland Oregon and exhibited it at Wieden+Kennedy's headquarters lobby. And in December, we even took the exhibition to Las Vegas as part of the huge

Autodesk University conference. We went on to travel the show to San Francisco and Chicago as well.

I proposed an exhibition called *Better Business by Design*—remember one of our first gigs was to help DIGMA produce an exhibition at their inaugural event at Reebok's headquarters, called *Design Means Business?* That exhibition in October 2010 was a success but was only up for that one-day event—folks would often ask us when that content was coming back. My idea was similar to Sarah's—we wouldn't have much capacity after *Street Seats,* and we needed quick wins. We had all the content from the 2010 exhibition, and it wouldn't take much effort to curate additional stories of design making an impact in business.

In July 2014, we opened *Better Business by Design* within Boston's newly renovated Innovation & Design Building. We partnered with the Design Management Institute to bring even more data and information to the show, depicting how businesses that adopt design do way better than those that don't.

Derek was very attuned to the advances in 3D printing and was always down to make design accessible to the masses. He proposed a design competition, fashion show, and exhibition called *Rapid Jewelry.* The idea was to put a design challenge out there, similar to *Street Seats,* but at a smaller scale. Derek's idea was to make 3D-printing more accessible by pairing it with something completely known by the public, jewelry.

In February 2015, we launched the *Rapid Jewelry* design challenge to design a piece of wearable jewelry, anything, as long as it was 3D-printed. We partnered with Solidscape who facilitated printing some of the pieces in silver—which was so amazing—and in May 2015, we unveiled the finalists with an incredible fashion show at the Boston Park Plaza Hotel. We

Dancers from Urbanity Dance modeling 3D-printed jewelry at the Rapid Jewelry Fashion Show, 2015. Photo: Chris McIntosh

One of the Design for Dining custom tables at The Merchant in Boston, designed by Payette Architects, 2015.

worked with a group of dancers as models to create a unique
experience. The dancers wove in and out of the crowd with
their 3D-printed jewelry. Later in September, we exhibited the
jewelry at the gallery at Boston Architectural College, and in
March 2016, we produced another fashion show and
exhibition at Portland's Hotel Lucia.

Scott Reilly proposed an idea to similarly show the public
design's connection to everyday life. Scott had developed this
idea over a few years: a way to show the world how the dining
experience is designed and how that experience has changed
through the decades. Scott's idea was for an exhibition with a
series of experiential vignettes, one from each decade, where
you could sit for a meal and see and feel the design around
you. In true Design Museum fashion, we turned the idea
inside out.

We often talked about how our museum collection was
already out in the world, and we just needed to help folks see
it. Instead of a gallery exhibition, we did something pretty
neat. We paired seven restaurants with seven different design
firms and a simple design brief: create a new dining experience
in a part of the restaurant. I still don't know how we convinced
the restaurants to go along with us on this, except they were all
trying to increase foot traffic. The design firms each took over
a part of the restaurant, designing a new table, chairs, lighting,
and menus. The chefs collaborated by creating new dishes and
drinks.

In June 2015, we launched *Design for Dining* at seven
restaurants in Boston's Downtown Crossing with seven
pairings: Legal Crossing and Bergmeyer Architects, Sip Wine
Bar and Gate 3 Design, jm Curley and IDEO, Silvertone and
STA, The Merchant and Payette Architects, Bonapita and
Soldier Design, and MAST' and Nelson. Of course, in front

of each restaurant was one of our Beacon signs—reused from *Street Seats* but with new content about *Design for Dining*—and a map of all seven restaurants. We had a few epic restaurant crawls that year, and some of the dining experiences are still within the restaurants to this day.

David Silverman is an architect and urban designer who spends a lot of time thinking about how cities can be better designed. David was fascinated by large-scale hack-a-thons happening in cities (basically large groups of people coming together, forming teams, and creating projects in real time to make an impact in cities). His proposed idea was to create an *Urban Innovation Festival* in Boston. We found the perfect venue and opportunity in what we ended up calling the *Neighborhood Border Zone*, a swath of land under the Interstate-93 overpass at the intersection of four Boston neighborhoods. The area under the overpass was dirty and dangerous, but people walked through it every day.

In July 2016, our Vice President Liz Pawlak led the production of the *Urban Innovation Festival* with teams of designers creating urban interventions and getting feedback from the public. We didn't do this multi-day brainstorming and design project in a conference room somewhere. We did it right under the overpass. The results were some amazing ideas to transform that space into a place for people to enjoy. And now, thanks to some forward-thinking landowners and city officials in Boston, that same area under the highway is a public park with beautiful art throughout.

The other idea I proposed was inspired by an article in *The Atlantic* titled *The Overprotected Kid*. When I read Hanna Rosin's piece, I knew I had to do something. In it, she writes, "A preoccupation with safety has stripped childhood of independence, risk-taking, and discovery—without making it

PlayCubes installation in Boston's Chinatown Park, designed by Richard Dattner, manufactured by Playworld, 2016.

safer." The solution she proposed was more play and better playgrounds. The design of playgrounds at the time, and for decades, made play worse. I thought of my childhood and how my brother Steve and I had so much unsupervised play. I can draw a straight line between my experience playing as a kid and the risk-taking, design, and entrepreneurial person I am today. I proposed an exhibition highlighting great playground design around the world and sharing the science behind the importance of outdoor play for a child's development.

This idea became our *Extraordinary Playscapes* exhibition and placemaking program which we launched in Boston in June 2016 at the Boston Society of Architects headquarters. Led by the amazing design curator, Amanda Hawkins, we developed a gallery exhibition featuring playgrounds from around the world, showing how they were designed and why they worked well for kids. We also had an epic timeline of the history of playground design and actual playable playground equipment—and the requisite floor padding—right in the show. But we didn't stop there.

Remember, our collection is already out in the world. We installed beacons at amazing playgrounds around Boston and published a *Playground Passport* so folks could visit great playgrounds in their city and learn who designed them, how, and why. In collaboration with Playworld, a major manufacturer of innovative playground equipment, we gifted two playgrounds to the city of Boston and installed them as part of the exhibition. We permanently installed a configuration of Richard Dattner's PlayCubes in Boston's Chinatown Park—an area of the city where kids never had a playground of their own. Richard designed the play cubes in the 1960s as modular dodecahedrons with holes cut in them that could be stacked in endless configurations—Playworld brought them back and modernized the design with incredible results.

We also temporarily designed Playworld's new Playform7 on Boston City Hall Plaza with a ribbon cutting with Mayor Walsh. Playform7 was a new playground designed around the very principles we were exhibiting, with opportunities for free play. Playform7 was then permanently installed in one of Boston's bordering neighborhoods. Extraordinary Playscapes represented the best of what Design Museum could be: gallery exhibitions, events, placemaking, and more.

We also held multiple kid workshops including one where city kids could build playground equipment from sticks and other natural materials. We traveled the city-wide exhibition to five more cities, Portland, San Francisco, Dallas, Seattle, and Chicago. In December 2017, the museum published a 200-page book by Amanda Hawkins and myself called *Design &*

Play, featuring all the research, content, and design work from the exhibition.

One meeting, six programs, five years. What's the lesson? Not that you should expect to have a Pixar-like idea lunch that generates four movie ideas and $1 billion at the box office. But when you do find the right mix of what you can do, what you like to do, what your customers want, and what your business model can support, don't be afraid to hit the gas and execute. We found traction with *Street Seats*. It hit on our mission to make design more accessible—public benches are pretty accessible. It engaged the creative community with the competition element, it inspired our audience, and we raised a lot of money to make it happen. Given its public nature, sponsors were excited to get involved, and our members loved seeing their support used to make the city a better place. That was the combination that got us traction.

Street Seats was so good, we even did it again, almost exactly the same way in the summer of 2018, but along the riverfront in Portland, Oregon. If you look at the six ideas that came out of the program committee meeting, they all had some mix of those same elements. We had made it, right? We hit the accelerator when we got traction, but we also knew to keep listening to our audience, learning, and pivoting to keep our business strong.

In late 2015 and early 2016, looking at our financials and cash flow, I started to get the feeling like something was wrong —or that something could go wrong. In collaboration with our Finance Committee Chair, Matt Edlen, we analyzed our finances to better understand our revenue streams related to our operations and programming. We found what was making me anxious: we were too reliant on corporate sponsorship as a revenue stream. In some years, it was over half of our revenue.

The bad feeling I was getting was amplified by imagining what would happen if that revenue dried up. What if something spooked corporate sponsors and the revenue stream went down? Say from, I don't know, a global pandemic or another recession?

Our reliance on corporate sponsors also made us think that the only way to grow was to do more programs so that we could raise more corporate sponsorship money. But this wasn't an efficient way to scale because we were spending most of the money we raised to produce the actual programs. Very little revenue overall was going toward operations, and even less was going toward growing operations and increasing headcount. This all led us to make two big changes.

First, we reorganized our budget to split revenue and expenses associated with programming and revenue and expenses associated with operations—we wanted to be able to see our financial picture clearly in those terms. We started forecasting revenue and expenses and tracking accounts monthly. This level of detail allowed us to see how changes we were making in our model were affecting the business much sooner than in quarterly or annual reports.

Second, we began work to diversify our revenue streams. Another board member, David Morgan, joined up with a lot of experience in philanthropy from his time at the Perkins School for the Blind. When he looked at our budget, he found that we had very little revenue coming from major donors— folks giving $500, $1000, or more—simply to support the organization. That was how we could diversify: increase the percentage of revenue coming from major donors. But how?

David was keen on us rethinking how we talk about what we do at the Design Museum and, thus, rethinking what we do. I hope you're seeing the theme here—I needed help. So I asked for it. I convened a group of board members, council members, and staff to think through our mission and how we could better position ourselves and our messaging to appeal to major donors without sacrificing our foothold in the corporate sponsorship world.

I asked one of our council members, Caleb Dean, to lead the multi-session workshop. Caleb is a master facilitator, big thinker, coach, and entrepreneur himself—he and his wife run a handful of natural product retail stores in the Boston area. We began the sessions mapping our approach and our programs to the impact we hoped to make. David stressed that donors were looking to make an impact—what was our impact? That work led us to rewrite our mission to what it is today: to bring the transformative power of design everywhere. We also paired off to think through how we could best build off this mission to connect with donors. Lucky me, I got paired with Caleb—a master at asking questions and ideating solutions.

Caleb asked me what sort of response I received from donors in the past who had rejected our pitches. I shared a real story with him. I met with a potential donor, a senior architect at a local firm, and I pitched the Design Museum for his personal support. I shared our programs, and he was interested, but he informed me that he only gives to support healthcare organizations—that's where his passion was, so he decided not to give to the Design Museum. After my story, I told Caleb that I wished I had a deck of cards with various design case studies on them, including stories of design making a major impact in healthcare. Jokingly, I said I would have taken that health card and slid it across the table so he could see that supporting the Design Museum meant also supporting better outcomes in healthcare. Caleb laughed and loved the story and said, "Well, you should make that card deck." So I did. After the meeting, I made a mock-up of the cards, all with stories from past exhibitions: one for healthcare, one for sustainability, one for play, and one for business. I even printed them out on nice heavy card stock and cut them out so I could feel them in my hands—there was something here.

Around this same time, I was finishing my MBA at Babson College where I chose to do my capstone project on Harvard Business Publishing, publishers of Harvard Business Review (HBR). I was fascinated by their business and operating models. Every business thought leader wanted to be published in HBR—there was a sort of draw for expert content creators because of the esteem of being chosen. Because of this, HBR became one of the best places to read business thought leadership across a number of areas, including strategy, innovation, marketing, finance, and more.

It got me thinking that if donors are focused on impact, we should be focused on the impact of design. I had my four prototype cards, and I went back and analyzed every event, exhibition, and educational program we had ever done and tried to categorize the most impactful ones. I got to twelve categories, which I called our twelve *Impact Areas:* Vibrant Cities, Healthcare, Social Impact, Workplace Innovation, Play, Sustainability, Education, Data Visualization, Entrepreneurship, Diversity, Business, and Civic Innovation.

I presented this concept to the team and the board—they loved it. We needed a framework, not only for our donor-focused messaging but for our programming as well. The six ideas that came out of the programming committee meeting were great, but we decided to do them purely because they met our mission, and we all liked them. But now we had a framework, an organizing principle, for every event, exhibition, and piece of content. We could ask: does it meet our mission and fall within at least one of the impact areas? The impact areas helped with donors. They saw the list of twelve and immediately could find at least one that they connected with, and it worked for corporate sponsors as well!

The *Impact Areas* allowed us to widen our reach—all of a sudden, we weren't even using the word design when we connected with folks. Design means a lot of different things to a lot of different people, but if an employee at a potential corporate sponsor is interested in sustainability, then we can talk about making an impact in sustainability and how the museum's work supports that. Later, we can share that it was design all along!

The *Impact Areas* helped with something else that tied very closely to my MBA capstone project. We noticed that our membership levels were sort of plateauing. When we spoke with members who were canceling, or considering canceling, they mentioned that they loved what we did, but they might only be able to come to one event or one exhibition per year. We needed a more regular benefit—especially as a museum that you couldn't just go visit whenever you wanted. Things just clicked in my mind. I decided to launch *Design Museum Magazine* as a quarterly print publication we would send to our members every three months—filled with what I called *Design Impact Stories,* case studies of how design made an impact in one of our design impact areas.

We launched the first issue of *Design Museum Magazine* in October 2016 to line up with our *Extraordinary Playscapes* exhibition opening in Portland. The cover story was about a playground design by Sasaki. They shared their approach to research-based play-focused design. The magazine was a huge hit with our members and became the number one reason new members joined the museum. Some people thought I was crazy to launch a print magazine in 2016, what with decades of the Internet making print magazines go out of business. But it was different for us. We were a museum without a building, so we needed something physical—a way for our audience to literally touch and hold the museum in their hands.

The magazine became the physical manifestation of our virtual museum. One of our board members held the first issue and remarked, "Okay, now we have something." The magazine became the thread that tied our entire approach together. It even opened up a new revenue stream with advertising. The magazine gave us an outlet and space to explore all twelve *Impact Areas,* giving us the leeway to focus our exhibitions and events on the most impactful design—to do the most *good* and attract major donors to our cause. This approach kicked off a whole new slate of impactful public design programming.

Braden Leonard sharing his designs for custom prosthetic devices at the Bespoke Bodies exhibition in Portland, OR, 2018.

During the run of *Extraordinary Playscapes* in Portland, our main contact at the Pacific Northwest College of Art, Mack McFarland, asked me how we decided what exhibition topics we focused on. Luckily, I had my answer in the twelve *Impact Areas,* and I shared that our exhibitions focus on the most impactful design for people, businesses, and the planet. He asked if we ever thought about doing an exhibition on prosthetic design. He knew folks coming back from conflict in the Middle East with prostheses, and he researched a lot of the advances in prosthetic design, including 3D printing and integrated sensors. My first thought was, what design is more impactful than the design you attach to your body? I also knew many of the Boston Marathon bombing survivors were getting specialized care and new prosthetic devices. Mack had funding for such an exhibition and asked if Design Museum would produce and travel a show. After connecting with the team, I agreed.

In February 2018, we premiered our new exhibition, *Bespoke Bodies: The Design & Craft of Prosthetics,* at PNCA—our first exhibition to launch in Portland. Over the next few years, we took it to multiple venues in Boston and Hartford, CT. And in December 2020, we published another book by Amanda Hawkins and myself with the same title—a book containing all the research, historical timeline, and stories of design impact from the exhibition.

Our vice president, Liz Pawlak, and I would often talk about how we found design as a career—it wasn't easy for either of us, and it involved a lot of luck. It's true for so many designers—you don't know or realize that you can build a career in the creative industries. This was a passion for Liz. She wanted to make it easier for young people to find design and become designers. So around mid-2015, we started developing an exhibition called *Inspiring Careers,* about the many different careers one can go into with a focus on design —the goal was for young people to see they could have a future in the creative industries.

We began work on *Inspiring Careers,* but in 2016, we heard from our audience and our donors: folks were asking what Design Museum was doing around diversity, equity, and inclusion. It was a lunch conversation—I am a big proponent of team lunches. We were talking about *Inspiring Careers,* and our exhibitions manager, Amanda Hawkins, had an amazing idea to evolve our concept into an exhibition featuring not only the careers open to those in design, but to do it by featuring women, people of color, and individuals from a variety and diversity of backgrounds and lived experience working in those careers.

With the help of our content advisory committee, we renamed the program *We Design,* and in October 2019, we premiered the exhibition at Boston's Boling Municipal Building in Roxbury, with over thirty profiles of incredible designers working in a wide array of fields. I attended the *We Design* opening reception with my mom, Wendy, who supported me in becoming a designer. While we were setting up, three Black teenagers came through, their eyes wide. They asked me what this was. I told them it was an exhibition about different jobs you could get as a designer. Within their view, they could easily see examples of three Black designers—one in footwear, an architect, and someone who designed robotics. They told me they never knew you could get a job designing shoes, buildings, or robots.

I brought them over to a table where we had postcards showing the different types of design you could go into, including arts & apparel, community, spatial, systems &

Sabrina Dorsainvil standing next to her exhibit at the We Design exhibition in Boston, 2019.
Photo: Eriola Kapaj

strategy, graphics, objects, and media & technology. The young men each took one of every single postcard, thanked me, and said they'd be back to see the whole exhibit. I turned and my mom was in tears—she knew my whole journey and knew this one interaction embodied everything I was doing at the Design Museum to make design more accessible to everyone, everywhere.

We traveled *We Design: People. Practice. Progress.* to multiple venues around Boston, including Boston City Hall in February 2020, and that same month, we opened the show in Portland Oregon. We took this concept a step further, and under the leadership of our Director of Learning & Interpretation, Diana Navarrete-Rackauckas, we developed a youth design education program. We partnered with Cambridge Public Schools to offer an after-school program where teens were paid to design solutions for their communities. We called it the *Neighborhood Design Project* and connected with hundreds of teens over the course of two years.

———

I'm incredibly proud of this work. We took our concept for a nomadic museum, made design accessible to all, and listened to our advisors and audience. We made our approach work for them, and we worked hard to make it real, so it's no surprise our audience was happy! After *Street Seats*, and after my TEDxBoston talk, which was seen by hundreds at the event and thousands online, people would often say to me, "Sam, you made it!" "No," I'd reply, "*We* are making it, every day." We built a culture of collaboration, adaptability, and reinvention. Even as we grew, we never lost the startup mentality of working hard and delivering for our audience in a changing world.

Never was that more apparent than in March 2020 when the COVID-19 pandemic hit the United States and disrupted literally everything. Our culture of reinvention put us right back in startup mode—one difference this time around is we had a dedicated team of full-time professionals. We immediately converted all our in-person events in Boston and Portland to virtual event experiences. We actually had a virtual event in March to test our approach, and it worked great.

For about a year prior to COVID, we worked with a group of board and council members to rebrand the museum as a national and global brand for design content and education. COVID gave us the push. As the pandemic swelled, we immediately rebranded our national organization from Design Museum Foundation—a brand we rarely used in public—to

Design Museum Everywhere, signaling that we were the design museum that comes to you, no matter where you are, anywhere in the world. We launched a brand video showcasing our offerings, including virtual events, print and online *Design Museum Magazine* issues, online education resources for kids, and more. And in April 2020, we launched our podcast, *Design is Everywhere*, a weekly show I hosted on the impact of design. With the leadership of our writer and producer Amor Yates, we produced over 100 episodes and quickly rose to be in the top twenty-five design podcasts in the U.S.

After the horrible tragedies following the murders of Ahmaud Arbery, Breonna Taylor, and George Floyd, and the following social movement for racial equity and liberation, we responded by bringing our entire *We Design* exhibition online, opening up the content to everyone. Diana led the creation of a curated list of anti-racism resources for designers, and we dedicated an entire issue of *Design Museum Magazine* to understanding the connection between design, race, and policing, under the thoughtful editorial leadership of Jennifer Rittner.

In the summer of 2020, as all these pivoted and relevant programs inspired and educated our audience, one of our board members, Elizabeth Lowery, reached out for a phone call. She wanted to congratulate me and the team for such a successful transformation in response to the changing world around us, and she wanted to know how Design Museum always had something going on to connect with the major ideas, shifts, and challenges facing our world. My answer was simple: our community.

The Russian-American management thinker and mathematician, Igor Ansoff, often spoke about weak signals of change, basically saying that the future is out there, but the signals are weak. You have to look and listen closely to identify them, and when you find them, you can see the future. Well, we had a signal amplifier: our community. We constantly and intentionally listened to our community to understand what they were thinking about, what they cared about, and what they were wondering about. And then we did those things, and we did them well. This isn't an approach that only a nonprofit museum can take to ensure success—any business can have an audience community and/or a community of advisors.

Pixar has this. too. They call it The Pixar Braintrust—a group of talented storytellers who trust each other enough to give real, candid feedback and make their movies better. Ed Catmull, president of Pixar Animation, wrote about the braintrust in his book, *Creativity, Inc.* The Braintrust developed in 1994 out of the rare working relationship between the five men closely working on the production of *Toy Story.* They trusted each other, listened to each other, and built off each other's ideas. The group grew as more directors and writers got involved at Pixar—to this day, they meet every few months to discuss and solve problems around each movie they're making. The Braintrust is credited with helping make films like The Incredibles, Up, and WALL-E the best they could be and the successes they are. As Ed wrote, "You don't have to work at Pixar to create a Braintrust. Every creative person can draft into service those around them who exhibit the right mixture of intelligence, insight, and grace."

Every single one of our programs from the *Urban Innovation Festival* and *Design for Dining* to *Extraordinary Playscapes* and *We Design* was born out of conversations with our community and developed in collaboration with groups of advisors steeped in expertise in the areas we sought to explore. It's all about people and trust. Derek and I, and the entire Design Museum team, trusted our community and advisors to engage and help. We just had to admit we didn't have all the answers, listen, and act.

CONCLUSION

"Entrepreneurship is living a few years of your life like most people won't so that you can spend the rest of your life like most people can't."
— Anonymous

Entrepreneurship is hard—it's the extreme sport of the business world—and it will take everything you have to succeed. But life is way too short to not start your entrepreneurial adventure. As Oliver Burkeman wrote in his book, *Four Thousand Weeks: Time Management for Mortals,* we have only about 4,000 weeks of life to do what we want to do. Life is too short to have any regrets, like not taking a chance on yourself and your ideas. As I reflected on my decision to take this chance, to start something that made a real impact in people's lives, I keep coming back to the incredible community around me, including my family, friends, the Design Museum team, and everyone involved—for me, it's these people and our experiences together that made this adventure so great.

This book is my entrepreneurial story, but it can be yours as well—or something like it. I truly believe you can start your business with nothing more than your idea, your time, and your grit. But to survive and succeed, you need to embrace change, try things, learn, and most of all, you need good people around you, a community of support. Creative startups are unique undertakings. The solution, approach, and business model aren't always obvious—there was no rule book for starting a nomadic design museum. There's likely no rule book for your business, but I hope this book you're holding serves as a guide.

You need people, but you are the first customer of your own idea—what are you going to do to convince yourself to buy in? Don't just think about it—our minds are filled with self-doubt. You need to get your idea out of your head. Make your business real somehow. Make a prototype of it just for you. You don't need to show anyone else at first. This is highly personal, and that's okay. I prototype so many businesses for myself—most of those prototypes help convince me not to move forward. A few prototypes panned out, including this book.

Once you've convinced yourself, I'm going to challenge you to convince at least one other person to buy all the way in and join you on this journey. If you can't convince just one person to join you, how are you going to convince hundreds, thousands, or millions to buy what you're selling? They'll be your co-founder—and trust me, you're going to need that unconditional support when times get tough and to celebrate with when you both win. Then go beyond two people. Every business needs a community to be successful. It can be ten people or 10,000, but you need a base of folks who are more than customers. You need supporters. At the Design Museum, we have concentric circles of community around us—there's the team, the board of directors, our council, the various content advisory committees helping us generate great content and public programming, our donors, members, and our global audience. Engaging with, listening, and acting in concert with all these groups was and is vital to our success. The market dynamics of brand affiliation, conscious consumption, and social media have changed the relationship between business and customer. Perhaps in the past, it was a one-way relationship. Now, for successful businesses, it's two-way—both business and customers learning from each other, providing value to one another, and growing together.

Know now that not everyone is going to want to join your community, and not everyone is going to love what you're doing. You don't want to surround yourself with a community of people who agree with you all the time—there's no innovation without creative conflict—but watch out for the naysayers. Some will actively try to convince you to stop. They'll say that you can't do it, or they may even work against you. If you have a strong community around you, it's easier to break through the naysayers, but I found it's also good to have your responses ready for them. Write them down, and have them on the tip of your tongue. You're going to need them.

Change is the only constant in life, and the same is true of business. Learn to love it. Live in the change. Don't let ownership of your idea cloud the need to listen to others, pivot, and adapt. Initially, in my mind, the Design Museum was going to be a building in downtown Boston. The economy, the market, our competitors, and even our early community members had something to say about that—we had to think differently and get creative in how we were going to make the impact we wanted to make and generate revenue at the same time. The best way you can address change is to be constantly listening and learning. There are so many resources available to learn anything and everything you'll ever need in your business—my two favorites: books and other people. If you want to learn from someone, reach out. That goes for me, too —I have public office hours set up on my website for this purpose. Distribute your ignorance across many sources and connections, then learn, try, apply, and repeat.

One thing you do not need to do is leave your nine-to-five job to start your business—at least, not at first. A popular mythological character is the entrepreneur who goes all in, risking everything to start their company. That's not an entrepreneur; that's a gambler and a bad one at that. As Justin Welsh often says, use your day job as startup capital for your new venture. That's what I did. Over the course of three years, I went from fully employed in a corporate job to slowly stepping down my job commitments, including teaching part-time, freelancing, and contracting, while building up the museum to the point where it could pay me a salary.

There are things you can do to help ensure survival and accelerate success. How you present business matters. First impressions matter, and, as we all know, you never get a second chance to make a first one. So make your business look and feel bigger and more established than you really are. That means designing and deploying a brand, logo, website, and print materials that look legit. If you're not a designer, hire one to elevate your presentation. A great brand that's bigger than your current state is a giant magnet that will pull you to the future state.

You must also identify and make opportunities—some opportunities will find you, but for the most part, it's your responsibility to generate them. Derek and I always took an approach of finding overlapping opportunities, meaning opportunities or projects that did multiple things at once and turned everyone involved into a winner. Look at the exhibition design course we taught, which was a win for the students, the school, the museum, and the general public. We were paid to teach an exhibit design course where we made the goal to produce a real exhibition for the Design Museum. The students got a real-world education, and the museum gained a public program. How can you water two (or three or four or five) plants with one hose? Find the connection points, and stretch your effort so that the outputs satisfy multiple needs or challenges. If you get it right, it's like cloning yourself, or getting two times the success for the same amount of effort— and you need those kinds of numbers in the early days.

Figure out your business model. How are you going to make money from this venture in a way that's fair to you and your customers and generates enough profit to go beyond survival and into growth and success? You can prototype business models just like you can prototype anything else. Keep trying things, experimenting, and building on what works. And when you've found that magic combination of product, customers, and business model—hit the gas, take some big swings, and test yourself and your business. Just like a great brand, a big project that takes your team and business outside the collective comfort zone can push you into a future state that's bigger than you could possibly imagine. Don't be afraid to think and act big—just do it in a way that doesn't endanger your current state. That's your fallback position. When you think you've made it, the market or the world will change— and you'll have to change with it—so stay in the present tense. You're making it, every day. Entrepreneurship is patience and impatience rolled into one. It's a marathon and a sprint at the same time—either way, you're running. Keep going.

You have a creative idea inside you—something that could bring joy, utility, and change to a world in desperate need of all three. It's not doing anyone any good living in your mind. You need to get it out, share it with yourself and others, then build from there. It's going to be hard. You're going to stumble, fall, and want to quit—I know I did at times. But the beauty in the adventure of starting something from nothing is in the things you learn, the relationships you build, and the impact you make together. Looking through that lens, every attempt is a success.

I'll leave you with the words my father often said to me, over and over during my forty years on this planet, words that helped steel me for a life of learning, trying new things, and creating value for others: *you can do anything you set your mind to.* He was right. Not just about me, but about everyone, including you.

You can do this.

Now go. Start.

ACKNOWLEDGEMENTS

I found so much joy while reminiscing about 13 years of starting, growing, and stewarding the Design Museum community. I am grateful to every volunteer, staff member, council member, board member, and supporter. If you ever put on the orange volunteer shirt at a Design Museum exhibition or event, thank you—this story wouldn't be possible without you.

I hope you gather from my entrepreneurial adventure that starting a business takes partnership and community. At three critical stages of development, I had terrific partners at the Design Museum. Derek Cascio co-founded the museum with me—Derek's heart and genius created the foundational values and approach that make the museum an extraordinary place and community. Liz Pawlak was the Vice President at the museum for six years—with her talents in design, business, and community-building, she grew the museum into what it is today. Maria Villafranca started as the museum's Marketing

Director, then Deputy Director, and now she runs the museum as the Executive Director. With her expertise in nonprofit leadership, design, and social impact, she's building the future of Design Museum Everywhere. Thank you Derek, Liz, and Maria!

Thank you to my wife Nicole for always being in my corner and creating space for me to write these words in our three-kid-chaotic life.

I had a fantastic editing team to help me turn these thousands of words into something coherent and useful. Thank you to Sara Stibitz and her team, including Faith Smith-Place, for working closely with me on this book.

I had an idea after writing Chapter 8 about Continuum designing the museum's logo in full public view. I approached my friends (and long-time supporters of the Design Museum) Blake Goodwin and Paul Reiss, founders of Proportion Design, a branding and design agency, to see if they would be up for designing the cover of this book and making the public part of the process. Fortunately for me, they were—they added Andrea Cincotta to the design team, and together, we created an 8-episode limited-series podcast chronicling their design process called *Inside Front Cover*. My friends Debbie Millman, Deb Aldrich, and Sarah Fonder at PRINT Magazine published each step of the design process on Printmag.com (thank you!). You can listen to the episodes on Apple Podcasts or Spotify; you'll find the links on my website, samaquillano.com. Big thanks to this team and everyone who shared their feedback on the cover design—you're holding the result!

You're also holding the result of an entrepreneurial, self-publishing effort. *Adventures in Disruption* exists because 137 backers successfully funded it on Kickstarter in October 2023.

Thank you to all my backers — I appreciate you! Special thanks to all my Book Patrons, including Allison Scott, José dos Santos, Dave Fustino, Deco Goodman, and John Doll. And extra special thanks to:

Sam & Wendy Aquillano, my parents, who are always there for me. My mom was there to help set up for our launch event, and my dad helped Derek and I build the Getting There exhibition; together, they were consistently two of our biggest supporters at the museum—I could go on and on. They made me, they made me who I am, and supported me every step of the way, and they still do. Thank you, Mom and Dad!

Kari Iverson is my friend from design school at RIT—Kari was a key team member of the *Thought at Work* student design conference we created. She designed and runs her own business, HELLO MODERN, where she does massage therapy to help those with chronic conditions in and around Mill Valley, CA. We reconnected while I was writing this book, and Kari consistently encouraged me to share my story and thought leadership—I know she's an avid reader of my *Business Design School* newsletter. Thank you, Kari!

David & Felice Silverman are design thought leaders who own and run STA Design, a collaborative architecture and interior design studio in Boston. David and Felice got involved with Design Museum Boston as we ramped up our placemaking efforts in the Fort Point area and launched our Center for Workplace Innovation. David is an amazing advocate for more human, environmentally connected cities, and Felice is an expert in workplace design. Together, they contributed to so many museum efforts over the years. At one point, David chaired our Board of Directors, and Felice was a leader on our workplace design think tank. I'm so grateful to them both for believing in me and constantly showing up to make the museum what it is today. Thank you, David & Felice!

David Morgan is a business thought leader and management consultant. David joined the board of Design Museum Everywhere at such a critical time, as we were shifting our primary focus from transactional to philanthropic support. He brought his decades of nonprofit management experience and gave his help and advice so freely and generously. He successfully supported the museum as we moved from only selling memberships and sponsorships to acquiring financial gifts purely in support of our mission. On top of that, he's a mentor to me and always supports my projects—thank you, David!

Bernard Lebow is the founder and Chief Operating Officer at SignWorks Group, an innovative designer, maker, and provider of interior, exterior, and specialty architectural accents and signage to customers and clients across North America. When I first met Bernie and shared the idea of the Design Museum, he lit up—he loved the idea, and from that moment on, he was one of my and our biggest supporters. No matter what the program or campaign, Bernie was there for us. Thank you, Bernie!

Nino Clarkin is a partner at Edward Jones, where she leads Enterprise Design. She's truly the godmother of design at the firm, evangelizing the power of design and setting the conditions for design leaders like me to do our best work. Nino is one of my leaders, and I'm grateful to work in the organization she created and stewards daily. Nino is the kind of leader I strive to be: warm, enthusiastic, and authentic—she brings her humanity to the work while also striving for results. I'm grateful for the opportunities she generously provides for me and my team, and I'm so thankful for her support both inside and outside the company. Thank you, Nino!

Finally, I want to thank you, the reader. Thank you for going on this journey with me and spending your time with this story. It means a lot to me. I hope you'll stay in touch! If this story resonates or you have questions or feedback, reach out! You can connect with me and sign up for my *Business Design School* newsletter at my website, samaquillano.com. Thank you!

**BUSINESS
DESIGN
SCHOOL**

businessdesignschool.org

www.ingramcontent.com/pod-product-compliance
Lightning Source LLC
Chambersburg PA
CBHW071452140726
47997CB00005B/1696